Lourda
A Greek Family
Cookbook

With Stories of Growing Up Greek in America

Marina Kamilatos

Strategic Book Publishing

Strategic Book Publishing
An imprint of Strategic Book Group
P.O. Box 333
Durham CT 06422
www.StrategicBookGroup.com

ISBN: 978-1-60911-182-3

Printed in the United States of America

To my daughter, Elena, and her husband Frankie Kane. To my sons, Theo and Tony Procopos. To my grandsons, Nikolas and Xander. To my mother, Roxanne Kamilatos, and my brother and sisters. Dina, I miss you so much. To Peter and Mary Danos and to Evan. To my beloved father, Antonios Kamilatos, who taught me the love of Kefalonia, and to Yiayia.

Contents

Introduction

The inspiration for this cookbook stems from my early childhood memories of celebrating great Greek family feasts. Stimulated by my fascinating trips to Greece, my love for the country grew because of its deep-rooted history, and most of all from the fabulous cuisine found there.

Lourdas: A Greek Family Cookbook, is based on the living tradition of Greek cuisine, with unique real-life stories of growing up Greek in America, and a collection of family and restaurant recipes. This book will present an array of authentic recipes with impressive innovations from my restaurant. *Lourdas: A Greek Family Cookbook*, concentrates mainly on two specific regions of Greece, which were my parents' ancestral homes. Dishes are inspired from my father's island of Kefalonia, a once Venetian ruled island, and by the treasured recipes of the shepherd's cuisine from my mother's Macedonian heritage. I've realized the culmination of a life-long dream when I opened my restaurant, Lourdas Greek Taverna. The appetite for Greek food is growing, and I've brought the flavors of Greece to this country through my restaurant, and now this book. I have passionately created intensely tasty and healthy dishes. My recipes are made with basic, and always fresh, ingredients and generous helpings of faith and love. From appetizing starters such as *xtapodi salata* (grilled octopus with fresh field greens); *Macedonian melintzanosalata* (roasted eggplant dip with crushed walnuts); *spanakopita* (savory spinach pie); to lovely main courses such as *Kefalonitiki kreatopita* (Kefalonian meat pie); *pastitsada* (spicy beef with pasta in a tomato wine sauce); *arni me fassoulakia* (lamb in the pot with green beans); *garides Lourdas* (pan seared shrimp with chopped tomatoes and feta); to impossibly delicious classic Greek desserts such as *galaktobouriko* (luscious custard-filled phyllo pastry soaked in syrup); *karithopita* (nut lovers cake); *melomakarona* (honey-dipped cookies); *kourambiedes* (melt-in-your-mouth wedding cookies); and baklava cheese cake. As an experienced chef/owner of Lourdas, this cookbook is filled with signature recipes from my restaurant, along with perfected Greek recipes with personal cooking tips.

Acknowledgments

To my daughter, Elena, thank you for all your precious time, patience, guidance, excellent suggestions, testing so many recipes, and teaching me how to write. Without you, this book would have never been written. To my son, Theo, thank you for taste testing and offering your expert opinions. To my son, Tony, thank you for helping me test and make recipes and for sharing your valuable cooking knowledge and culinary skills. But most of all, I thank you for believing.

1
Name Days

A Name Day Party at Yiayia's House

When I was a little girl, I couldn't wait until we went to my Yiayia's house for name day parties so I could watch her make big, savory pitas. Even then, I knew that one day I would master making pitas just like Yiayia. We celebrate name days. Most orthodox Greeks are named after a saint and on this saint's day, you celebrate your name day. A name day is like having a birthday party without the usual cake and candles, but perhaps a gift of food or wine. It is important to visit or at least call a person on his or her name day and wish them good health, happiness, and many years to come (xronnia polla). Those who come to visit, come to eat. My grandmother on my mother's side, Yiayia, came to America in 1925. Her name was Glykeria, though to her friends she was nicknamed Blaga. When she stepped ashore on Ellis Island, Yiayia carried in her head many of the recipes for the traditional foods of Macedonia. This, the birthplace of Alexander the Great and Aristotle, is known for its shepard's cuisine. The region is famous for its great pita recipes. Butter is used instead of olive oil, and Yiayia added butter to most of her recipes. Being so near the Balkan borders, the cuisine of Macedonia has a marked Slavic influence, with an added touch of its Turkish occupied past. Yiayia was from the town of Bitola, formerly called Monastir, a city in the southwestern part of the republic of Macedonia, not far from the town of Florina, where delicious red Florina peppers are farmed in the fertile valleys. Yiayia often roasted peppers on top of the stove and then seasoned them with olive oil, garlic, and vinegar. Yiayia was great at stuffing vegetables. She made delicious stuffed cabbage and stuffed peppers. Walnuts were often used in many dishes, like Yiayia's melintzanosalata. Now I know why Yiayia loved to make foods with these ingredients, these are the foods she grew up eating. Yiayia made pita in the traditional Macedonian way, kneading, buttering and stretching the dough with her *pita stick* (wooden dowel) until the dough looked like a giant pizza. I always tried to steal a piece of the raw dough to eat and, Yiayia always yelled at me for this. After making the dough, Yiayia filled the pitas with assorted savory fillings, such as spinach or leeks and cheese. *Praso pita* (leeks pita) was the best! After eating pita like this, you never forget how incredibly delicious it can taste.

My Grandfather, Papou Yorgos (named for St. George), celebrated his name day on April 24th. When we were young, Yiayia had plates of Greek candies and treats to keep us occupied at name day parties; sweets like *loukoumia* also called Turkish delight and snacks such as *stragalia* (dried salted chickpeas) mixed with raisins. Nobody ever went hungry at her home on a name day feast. Yiayia also had a band of allies to help on those festive occasions. All her lady friends would come over to take part. I remember their names still—Marika, Takiosh,

Youba, Margarita, Kitsa and Elpiniki. They all came dressed in their Sunday best, from hats to high heels. Like Yiayia, they all hailed from the old country and spoke several Slavic languages. Yiayia treated them to her special *quince spoon sweet* (kydoni glyko) which she served to each on her tiny crystal dishes, along with a cold glass of water which is needed after all the sugar. This is a standard Greek tradition when someone comes to visit. I can't remember a day going by, even when it wasn't a special occasion, that Yiayia wasn't cooking. I owe a lot to my Yiayia—she was my cooking teacher, my inspiration, and a major influence in my life. Without her, I wouldn't be where I am today.

YEMISTES PIPIERIES TSI YIAYIAS

Stuffed Peppers

Serves 8

This is one of my favorite recipes, one that Yiayia always prepared for a great family dinner. The fresh red bell peppers remind me of the peppers of Florina. To make this dish more colorful, I pair them with green bell peppers. In this recipe, the peppers are stuffed with a delicious mixture of meat and rice with herbs, and then baked along with potatoes in a flavorful tomato sauce. I like to bake the peppers until the tops are crisp, which makes them taste so good!

§ § § § § §

8 large bell peppers, a mixture of both red and green

3 tablespoons olive oil

1 pound lean ground beef

1 cup finely chopped onions

4 garlic cloves, minced

4 tablespoons tomato paste

2 cups vegetable stock

2 tablespoons butter

1 teaspoon salt

1/2 teaspoon pepper

1/2 teaspoon dried dill

2 teaspoons chopped fresh parsley

1 cup rice

3 large baking potatoes, peeled and quartered

For the Sauce:

3 tablespoons tomato paste

2 cups vegetable stock

3 garlic cloves, minced

3 tablespoons olive oil

1 teaspoon salt

1/4 teaspoon pepper

§ § § § § §

Rinse and dry the peppers. Slice off stem ends and reserve. Remove the seeds and cores.

Heat the olive oil in a large sauté pan over medium-high heat. Add the meat and brown until no longer pink. Add the onions and garlic and cook until softened, about 5 minutes. Add the tomato paste, stock, butter, salt, pepper, dill, and parsley. Stir to blend the flavors. Bring to a quick boil and simmer for 2 minutes. Add the rice. Remove the pan from heat and transfer the meat mixture to a bowl to cool. Preheat the oven to 375°F. Loosely fill each pepper with the stuffing. Top the peppers with the caps and arrange them in a large baking pan or casserole dish.

Make the Sauce: In a medium size bowl, dilute the tomato paste with the stock. Add the garlic, olive oil, salt and pepper. Pour the sauce into the baking pan or casserole dish with the stuffed peppers. Cover the pan with aluminum foil. Bake for about 1 hour. Remove the foil. Add the potatoes to the pan and continue baking 1 hour, basting the peppers every 15 minutes, until the peppers have begun to brown, and the potatoes are cooked through. Remove casserole dish from the oven. Place a pepper along with a few of the potatoes on individual serving dishes. Spoon some of the juices over the peppers. Serve immediately or at room temperature accompanied by feta with olives and plenty of fresh bread.

Note: Leftovers can be stored in the refrigerator for up to 2 days.

YOUVETSI

A Baked Casserole of Beef with Orzo Pasta

Serves 4

The dish takes its name from the clay pot, youvetsi. This is a method of cooking along with tomatoes and pasta which creates a lovely rich flavor. Serve immediately as the orzo absorbs much of the juices.

§ § § § § §

3 tablespoons olive oil

1 1/2 to 2 pounds boneless beef chuck, cut into 1 1/2 inch cubes

1 cup chopped onions

3 garlic cloves, sliced

2 cups crushed tomatoes

3 tablespoons butter

1 bay leaf

4 cups vegetable stock

Salt and pepper to taste

2 cups orzo pasta

Grated kefalotyri cheese or pecorino Romano, for garnish

§ § § § § §

Heat the oil in a large stewing pot over medium high heat. Add the meat and brown in batches if necessary, about 8 to 10 minutes. Add onions and garlic and sauté until soft, 5 minutes. Add the tomatoes, butter, bay leaf and 2 cups of the stock. Season the sauce with salt and pepper and stir to blend. Bring to a simmer and cook until the beef is almost tender, approximately 1 1/2 hours. Preheat the oven to 350°F. Remove the pot from the stove. Carefully transfer the beef to a deep casserole or baking dish. Add the orzo and 2 cups of the remaining stock and stir. Place the dish in the oven and bake for approximately 30 minutes or until the meat and pasta are tender. Remove the bay leaf. Serve right away on individual serving dishes. Garnish with shavings of kefalotiri cheese.

ARNI ME FASSOULAKIA

Lamb-in-the-Pot with Green Beans

Serves 4

In Greek cooking there is an array of "lamb-in-the-pot" meals. For this recipe, which is similar to a stew, the lamb, onions, and garlic are slowly cooked in a tomato sauce until the lamb is fork tender. Green beans are added near the end of the cooking. Frozen green beans work just as well.

§ § § § §

4 tablespoons olive oil

1 1/2 to 2 pounds bone-in lamb shoulder, or boneless lamb shoulder, cut into 1 1/2-inch cubes, rinsed and patted dry

1 cup chopped onions

4 to 5 garlic cloves, sliced

1 cup tomato sauce

1 cup chopped tomatoes or canned chopped tomatoes

2 cups vegetable stock or more

2 tablespoons butter

1 bay leaf

1 teaspoon salt

1/2 teaspoon pepper

1 pound fresh green beans

§ § § § §

Heat the oil in a large pot over medium-high heat until hot, but not smoking. Add the lamb and brown well on all sides, about 8 to 10 minutes. Add the onions and garlic and sauté until soft. Add the tomato sauce, chopped tomatoes, the stock, just enough to cover the lamb, butter, bay leaf, salt and pepper. Stir to blend. Cover and simmer until the meat is almost tender, approximately 1 hour. Add green beans and continue cooking for 20 minutes or until the meat and beans are tender and the sauce has slightly thickened. Taste and adjust the seasonings. Discard bay leaf. Serve the lamb with a portion of green beans and their cooking juices on individual serving dishes.

Kotopoulo me Fassoulakia

Variation: To make *kotopoulo me fassoulakia* (chicken with green beans) substitute a 2 1/2 to 3 pound chicken, cut into serving pieces. Prepare as above and cook for approximately 30 minutes, or until the chicken is almost tender.

KITHONI GLYKO

Quince Spoon Sweet

Makes 3 cups

Kithoni glyko is a homemade confection made from the fragrant quince fruit. It is a Greek custom to treat guests with a spoonful of glyko. In this recipe, the fruit is thinly sliced and simmered in sugar, flavored with cinnamon and clove that enhances the flavors to produce a deliciously sweet confection the consistency of slightly thickened Simple Syrup. It is usually followed with a cold glass of water and a cup of Greek coffee. I like to spread it on toast for breakfast like preserves. It's just delicious.

§ § § § §

1 pound quinces

2 cups water

2 tablespoons lemon juice

3 cups sugar

1 teaspoon light corn syrup

Sachet: 1 cinnamon stick, 2 whole cloves, plus the reserved quince cores and seeds, wrapped and tied up in piece of cheesecloth

2 to 3 rose geranium leaves (optional)

§ § § § §

Peel and core quinces. Cut quinces in half and julienne. Place them in a bowl of cold water with 1 tablespoon of the lemon juice until ready to cook. Drain the quinces and add them to a medium-sized pot with 2 cups of water and remaining tablespoon of lemon juice. Bring to a boil and cook, covered, over medium heat until soft, about 10 minutes. Add sugar, corn syrup, and the sachet and continue cooking, uncovered, over medium-high heat, to thicken, about 15 minutes. Add the rose geranium leaves and cook 2 more minutes. Remove from heat and discard sachet. Cool and pour in sterilized jelly jars.

Note: Store in the refrigerator for up to 2 months.

ARNI FRICASSE ME ANTITHIA

Lamb Fricassee with Escarole

Serves 4

In this flavorful dish, lamb is simmered along with scallions, onions, and escarole. At the end of the cooking, it is flavored with *Saltsa Avgolemono* (egg-lemon) sauce. You can simplify this dish by substituting chopped lettuce for escarole. This is best served as soon as it is made.

§ § § § §

1 pound fresh escarole

4 tablespoons olive oil

1 1/2 to 2 pounds lean boneless lamb shoulder, cut into bite size pieces, or bone in lamb shoulder, rinsed and pat dried

1/2 cup chopped scallions, white and light green parts

1 cup chopped onions

2 cups vegetable stock or more

1 tablespoon fresh chopped flat or curly parsley

2 teaspoons chopped fresh dill

2 tablespoons butter

Juice of 1/2 fresh lemon

Salt and white pepper to taste

2 cups Saltsa Avgolemono (see page 39).

§ § § § §

Rinse, drain, and separate the leaves of the escarole and set aside. Heat the oil in a large pot over medium-high heat. Add the lamb, scallions and the onions. Sauté, without browning, until soft, about 5 to 8 minutes. Add the stock, just enough to cover the lamb, parsley, dill, butter, lemon, salt and white pepper. Cover and simmer for 1 hour, or until the lamb is almost tender. Add the escarole and cook uncovered, 10 minutes or until the lamb is fork tender and the escarole is cooked. In the meantime, make the Saltsa Avgolemono. When the lamb is done, remove the pot from the heat. Very slowly pour the Saltsa Avgolemono over the lamb, shaking the pot until the sauce is thoroughly incorporated. Return the pot to the heat and simmer 5 minutes or until the sauce has slightly thickened. Serve a portion of the lamb along with the escarole and sauce on warm plates. Serve the remaining sauce on the side. Rice pilaf is a great accompaniment.

MAKEDONIKO SPANAKOPITA

Macedonian Spanakopita

Serves 8 to 10 (large servings)

Yiayia Making Pita

This is Greek soul food. Incredible layers of buttered phyllo dough, enveloped in a mixture of spinach and feta cheese. This is one of the more complex recipes in this book. For those willing to take the challenge of making homemade phyllo, I can assure you, it's quite worth the effort. I prefer to make phyllo using a thin wooden dowel which gives you more room for stretching the dough, but you can also use a rolling pin. Serve in large square pieces as a light lunch or accompanied with a Greek salad for dinner.

§ § § § §

For the Phyllo:

3 1/2 cups all-purpose flour, plus some for dusting the pastry board

1 to 1 1/4 cup warm water

1 teaspoon salt

2 tablespoons olive oil

2 tablespoons melted butter

2 tablespoons shortening (Crisco)

For the Spinach and Cheese filling:

2 (10-ounce) bags of fresh washed spinach, chopped

2 cups crumbled feta cheese

2 cups cottage cheese

4 eggs, beaten

2 teaspoons freshly chopped dill

A mixture of 1/2 pound (2 sticks) butter plus 1 tablespoon shortening (Crisco) melted for brushing

§ § § § §

To make the Phyllo: Place the flour in a large mixing bowl. Make a well in the center. Add 1 cup of the warm water, salt, olive oil, butter, and the shortening. Work the flour into the liquid with your hands, using more of the remaining water if needed until the dough begins to form. Turn the dough out on to a pastry board dusted with flour. Knead the dough for about 20 minutes, until it is smooth and elastic. Divide the dough into 12 golf-ball size pieces. Knead each piece of dough for about 2 minutes. Roll each piece out to resemble a circle, 1/4 inch thickness, and approximately 5-inch round. Lightly brush and stack one on top of another using 6 circles (don't butter the last one). Repeat with the remaining circles. Cover with plastic wrap and refrigerate for about 1 hour.

Make the Spinach and Cheese Filling: In a large bowl combine the spinach, feta cheese, cottage cheese, eggs and the dill. Mix well using your hands.

Preheat oven to 350°F. Butter an 18- by 14- by 1-inch baking pan and set aside. Remove the two stacks of buttered phyllo from the refrigerator. Sprinkle your work surface with a little flour. Using a rolling pin or wooden dowel, roll and stretch out one of the stacks of dough as thin as possible, carefully lifting it at times with your hands and fists. Lay the dough in the baking pan, allowing for the dough to over-lap along the edges of the pan by about 1 inch. Spread the filling evenly into the pan. Repeat rolling process for the second stack of dough, and place the dough evenly over the top of the filling, scrunching the dough gently all over to fit the pan. Roll and pinch in the edges to seal the crust. Brush all of the pastry with the remaining melted butter mixture. Prick the pie with a fork in several places. Bake for 50 minutes, or until the pastry is golden and puffy. Remove and let the pie cool in the pan. Serve warm.

Note: The dough can be wrapped and refrigerated for 2 to 3 days to give you a head start. Allow it to warm up to room temperature before using. It can also be wrapped and stored in the freezer for future use for up to one month. When ready to use, defrost in the refrigerator 24 hours, then let it warm up to room temperature two hours before using.

Variation: For *prasopita* (leeks pie), instead of spinach, substitute 8 medium-size leeks, white and light green tender parts only. Thinly slice and wash thoroughly, to remove all grit. In a large sauté pan melt 1 stick of butter over medium high heat. Add the leeks and cook until soft, about 10 minutes. Remove the pan from the heat. Place the leeks in a bowl and allow to cool. Omit the dill. Combine the feta cheese, cottage cheese and the eggs. Mix well and follow the directions above.

Variation: To make spanakopites, the triangle shape spinach pies that are real party pleasers, substitute 2 packages store bought phyllo pastry, preferably fresh, sold at Greek and ethnic specialty stores thawed according to the package instructions. Line 2 baking sheets with parchment and set aside. Preheat the oven to 350°F. Butter one sheet of phyllo at a time, keeping the unused portion covered with plastic wrap to keep it from drying out. Fold the sheet in half and butter again. Place one tablespoon of the spinach filling 1/2 inch from the narrow edge of the sheet. Brush with butter and fold up, as you would a flag, into a triangular shape. Place the triangle, seam-side down, onto the baking sheet. Repeat until all of the sheets are used. Brush the tops with butter. Bake for 1 hour, or until golden-brown. Remove and allow to cool a little. Place the spanakopites on a serving dish and serve immediately. Makes approximately 48 pieces.

Note: Spanakopites can be prepared and frozen unbaked. When ready to use, place unthawed in a preheated oven and bake 1 hour, or until golden.

MILOPITA ME STAFIDES

Greek Apple Pie with Golden Raisins

Serves 6 to 8

This is a simple dessert similar to apple strudel. A delicious filling of fresh sliced apples and golden raisins scented with cinnamon and spices rolled up in buttery sheets of flaky phyllo pastry and dusted with confectioners' sugar. A dollop of crème fraîche or ice cream pairs great!

§ § § § §

4 cups tart apples (4 apples peeled, cored and finely sliced)

1 cup firmly packed brown sugar

1 teaspoon cinnamon

1/2 teaspoon ground cloves

1 tablespoon flour

1 teaspoon vanilla

1/2 cup golden raisins

8 sheets phyllo pastry, at room temperature

2 sticks (1/2 pound) unsalted butter melted

1/2 cup confectioners' sugar for dusting

§ § § § §

Preheat oven 350°F. Line an 18- by 14- by 1-inch baking pan with parchment paper. In a medium size bowl combine the apples, sugar, cinnamon, cloves, flour, vanilla, and raisins. Toss to mix and set aside. Place one sheet of phyllo on a work surface with the longer edge facing you and brush with butter. Layer and butter the next three sheets, one on top of the other. Spread half of apple filling evenly to within one inch of all edges. Fold in one inch on both sides and roll up, like a jelly roll. Brush with butter. Using both hands, gently scrunch the roll gently together, to resemble a wrinkled roll. Repeat for second roll. Place, seam side down, on the baking pan and bake 30 minutes, or until golden brown. Transfer to a rack and let cool until warm. Dust with confectioners' sugar. Slice and place on individual dessert plates.

Note: Why not make two rolls at the same time and freeze for future use. Wrap with plastic wrap and place the unbaked roll in the freezer. When ready to use, remove from the freezer and bake, unthawed at 350°F for 35 to 40 minutes, or until golden brown.

Variation: Make a great, in-a-hurry dessert. Substitute canned apple pie filling and add raisins. It works great.

MELINTZANOSALATA

Eggplant Dip with Walnuts

Serves 2 to 4

This is a delicious vegetarian eggplant dip. A rustic combination of roasted eggplant, red peppers, olive oil, garlic and vinegar makes this taste so good. The addition of crushed walnuts suggests its Macedonian origin. This dip is similar to baba ghannoush.

§ § § § § §

1 medium eggplant (about 1 pound)
2 tablespoons extra virgin olive oil
1/2 teaspoon salt
1 small red bell pepper, roasted, peeled and chopped
5 cloves garlic, minced
2 teaspoons red wine vinegar
1/2 cup crushed walnuts (optional)
Fresh mint sprigs for garnish

§ § § § § §

Preheat oven to 375°F. Pierce the eggplant in several places with a knife. Rub the eggplant all-over with 1/2 teaspoon of the olive oil. Place the eggplant on a baking sheet and roast in the oven until the eggplant has collapsed, about 1 hour. Remove the eggplant from the oven and place into a colander to drain until all the juices run out, about 1/2 hour. Slit the eggplant lengthwise and scrape the pulp into a medium size bowl. Whisk the pulp with a fork or a wire whisk. Add the remaining olive oil, salt, red peppers, garlic and vinegar to the eggplant and stir until blended. Add the crushed walnuts if using. Chill in the refrigerator. Place the egg-plant in a chilled serving bowl. Garnish with fresh mint sprigs and serve chilled accompanied by warm pita wedges or fresh bread for dipping.

TARATORE

Cold Cucumber Soup

Serves 4

This is the refreshing soup that Yiayia made for us on hot summer days. A popular soup made in the Northern parts of Greece and Balkan countries. It is so simple and easy to make. Yogurt is the basic ingredient for this soup, but Yiayia always substituted it with buttermilk which gave it a distinctive creamy texture complemented by the fresh flavors of garlic, cucumbers and crushed walnuts.

§ § § § §

1 cucumber, peeled, seeded and finely diced
1 quart chilled buttermilk
3 cloves garlic, minced
Salt and pepper
1/3 cup olive oil
White vinegar for drizzling
1/2 cup crushed walnuts for garnish

§ § § § §

In a large bowl combine the cucumber, buttermilk, garlic, salt, pepper and olive oil. Stir until blended. Taste for seasonings. To serve, divide soup among chilled serving bowls. Drizzle with vinegar and garnish each with walnuts.

PIPIERES PSIMENES ME LADI

Roasted Peppers with Olive Oil

Serves 4 to 6

Traditionally in Florina, these delicious roasted sliced peppers are a part of the *mezé* (appetizer) course. A perfect starter simply flavored with plenty of olive oil, garlic, and vinegar which gives them a robust flavor. You can substitute green bell peppers or use both for added color and flavor. They are a great accompaniment to an hors d'oeuvres platter along with feta cheese and Kalamata olives or atop toasted baguette slices.

§ § § § § §

3 to 4 large red bell peppers
1 teaspoon vegetable oil
1 1/2 cups olive oil
6 cloves garlic, sliced,
3 tablespoons red wine vinegar
Salt and pepper to taste
Sprigs of fresh mint or cilantro for garnish

§ § § § § §

Wash and dry the peppers and place them into a large bowl. Using your hands, lightly coat them with the vegetable oil.

For gas stove-top method: Using tongs, place 2 peppers at a time on a medium-high open flame, turning peppers, until they are charred and soft. Remove with tongs and immediately rinse with cold running water. Peel away skins and remove stem and seeds with your hands. Drain and slice into thin strips. In a medium bowl combine peppers, olive oil, garlic, vinegar, salt and pepper. Toss to coat. Taste for seasonings. Place in a serving dish and serve room temperature or chilled garnished with fresh mint or cilantro sprigs.

For oven-roasting method: Preheat oven to 400°F. Place peppers on baking sheet and roast, turning frequently until charred and soft on all sides. Remove from oven and continue the recipe as above.

Note: The peppers can be refrigerated in a covered jar for up to 1 week. Cool to room temperature before serving.

DOLMADES

Stuffed Grape Leaves with Rice

Serves approximately 20 to 30 (about 5 dozen)

At my restaurant a customer once said, "These are the best dolmades I've had in about thirty years." Dolmades are a popular mezé item on most Greek menus that appear on the "pekelia," the assorted appetizer dish. These lovely leaves are stuffed with a mixture of rice, chopped onions and fresh dill. Then they are carefully rolled and nestled into a simmered pot, flavored with fresh lemon and extra virgin olive oil. It will take some patience and practice to learn how to roll these delicious dolmades, so you'll want to start making this recipe a day ahead and also to let the flavors mend. In Greece, freshly picked grape leaves are used, but since they are not readily available everywhere, substituting jarred grape leaves are much easier. They can be found at Greek and ethnic specialty stores.

§ § § § §

2 (1-pound) jars grape leaves

4 cups finely chopped onions

1 cup olive oil

2 cups rice

4 tablespoons freshly chopped dill

2 tablespoons freshly chopped flat leaf or curly parsley

2 tablespoons salt

1 cup fresh lemon juice

5 to 6 cups boiling water

Lemon wedges for garnish

Extra virgin olive oil for garnish

§ § § § §

Rinse grape leaves in cold water to remove the brine. Separate the leaves and cut off the stems. Save torn and thick leaves for lining the bottom and sides of a large pot.

Filling: In a large bowl combine the onions, olive oil, rice, dill, parsley, salt, and 1/2 cup of the lemon juice. Mix thoroughly.

Make the dolmades: Place one leaf at a time on a flat surface, shiny side down and place one tablespoon of filling at the bottom center. Fold in each side towards the center and roll up over the filling. Continue with the remaining leaves and place stuffed grape leaves in the pot tightly together, seam side down, in circular layers. Cover tightly with remaining leaves. Add the remaining lemon juice and enough water to just cover dolmades. Cover the pot, bring to a boil, then reduce heat and simmer for about 45 minutes, or until liquid is almost all absorbed. Uncover and cool completely in pot. Carefully remove the dolmades to a serving platter. Garnish with lemon wedges all around and drizzle with olive oil. Serve at room temperature or chilled.

Note: Keep extras covered and stored in the refrigerator for up to 2 days. Cool to room temperature or chill before serving.

LAHANO DOLMADES AVGOLEMONO

Stuffed Cabbage with Avgolemono Sauce

Serves 4

Cabbage is a favorite in Florina, Greece. This was one of Yiayia's favorite warm winter dishes when I was growing up. These rice and meat stuffed cabbage leaves with other flavorful ingredients are simmered slowly and become especially tender. The smooth and velvety Saltsa Avgolemono makes this dish just perfect. If savoy cabbage is not available, use green cabbage.

§ § § § §

1 tablespoon salt

1 head savoy cabbage, about 1 1/2 pounds

3 tablespoons olive oil

1 cup finely chopped onions

1 teaspoon minced garlic

1 pound lean ground beef

2 tablespoons tomato paste

1/2 teaspoon nutmeg

Salt and pepper to taste

1 teaspoon chopped fresh flat-leaf or curly parsley

1/2 cup rice

1 1/2 cups chicken stock

1 bay leaf

4 tablespoons butter

2 cups Saltsa Avgolemo (see page 39)

§ § § § §

Fill a large pot with water. Add the salt and bring to a boil. Ready a large bowl filled with ice and water. Add the cabbage too the pot and cook for about 10 minutes, or until tender. Remove the cabbage and plunge it into an ice bath to cool. Drain well in a colander. Heat the oil in a large skillet over medium-high heat. Add the onions and the garlic and sauté until soft, about 5 minutes. Add ground beef, stirring to break apart the meat. Sauté for about 5 more minutes, until the meat is lightly browned. Add the tomato paste, nutmeg, salt, pepper, parsley and the rice. Mix thoroughly and simmer for another 5 minutes. Taste for seasonings. Remove from the heat and spoon into a bowl to cool. Carefully cut away the core of the cabbage and separate as many leaves as possible without tearing. Save unused and torn leaves. Line the bottom of a large pot with a layer of these leaves, reserving the remainder for the top. Cut a V across the bottom of each leaf to remove the hard vein. Take one tablespoon of the stuffing mixture and place at the bottom center of the leaf. Roll over to cover the stuffing, and then turn in each side towards the center and continue to roll up tightly. If leaves are too big, cut them in half before rolling. Place the stuffed leaves in the pot, seam side down in a circular arrangement, keeping the layers tightly packed. Cover with remaining unused cabbage leaves, packing them down tightly. Add chicken stock to just about cover the layers. Add bay leaf and butter. Bring to a boil, then simmer covered until the cabbage is tender, about 1 hour. Place lahano dolmades on individual serving dishes. Spoon Saltsa Avgolemono over top and serve hot.

Note: Keep leftovers covered and stored in the refrigerator for up to 2 days.

Note: If there is not enough remaining leaves, place an inverted heatproof plate over the dolmades to keep them tightly together.

2

Growing Up Greek in America

Platanos

My father, Andonios Kamilatos, came to America in the early 1940s. Here, he met and married my mother Roxanne. I was born in Philadelphia 1953, just around the same time of the devastating earthquake of Kefalonia, which my father's mother Yiayia Anezina miraculously survived. Many islanders like my Yiayia left to begin a new life. Yiayia came to the United States on board the Queen Fredericka headed for New York in the 1960s to live with us. I grew up in a very closely-knit Greek community in the suburbs with my brother and sisters. My father always reminisced of Kefalonia and we were told countless stories of the *xorio* (the village) and how he would love for all of us to move back there. I was the one most affected by this, because this is a place where I always visit.

My father's side of the family also brought knowledge of the foods of their native region, the Ionian Islands. These seven islands off the western coast of Greece have acted as stepping stones down through the ages for Greeks heading to Italy and for Italians, especially the Venetians, traveling to Greece. As you might expect the food, including pita is very different from Macedonian recipes. As I grew older, I learned a lot about cooking from Yiayia and my parents. My father loved to cook. He loved to make *fakes* (lentil soup) and always had a secret ingredient that he added. We ate lots of fresh *horta* (field greens) and beans. My father also loved to make his special *halva* (farina dessert) for us. On Sundays my mother sometimes treated us to her famous *moussaka* (a casserole of eggplant, potatoes and beef), one of our family favorites. The most important thing was, as a Greek family, we always ate together. My parents constantly had the Greek music playing in the house. The sounds of Xiotis, Mary Linda, Stratos Dionisiou, and Tsitanis. Dad sat and strummed the guitar to the rhythm of the *Kandathes* (Kefalonian serenades) while mom did the dishes. I still remember all these artists and knew all the lyrics of the music by heart. Every Sunday, we took family trips down town to the Parras Greek store to buy some new 45's. My dad spoke only Greek to us. We ate Greek food, went to Greek functions, and of course, attended Greek school.

My father was a waiter most of his life. One day he opened up a restaurant in Kennett Square, PA. My sisters and I were in charge of the ice cream counter and small coffee station. We had so much fun working there. This is where I got my first real lessons in the restaurant business. Little did I know, this was only the beginning. I want to share with you some of the favorite dishes we ate while growing up.

FASSOULATHA

White Bean Soup

Serves 5 to 6

Fassoulatha is the most popular soup of Greece. This is one soup that is sure to warm your soul. Only a few inexpensive ingredients are needed for this hearty white bean soup recipe. Serve along with a Greek salad and plenty of fresh warm bread.

§ § § § §

1 cup dried white beans, northern or navy beans, soaked overnight in water and drained
2 quarts cold water
1 medium onion, coarsely chopped
1/2 cup coarsely chopped celery
1 clove garlic, peeled
1/4 teaspoon dried Greek oregano
1 bay leaf
2 tablespoons tomato paste
1 tablespoon olive oil
1/4 cup diced carrots
Salt and white pepper to taste
Extra-virgin olive oil for garnish

§ § § § §

In a large pot, combine the beans and water and bring to a boil. Add the onions, celery, garlic, oregano, bay leaf, and tomato paste. Reduce the heat to medium and cook for 1 hour. Add the olive oil and simmer for 30 minutes more. Add carrots, salt and pepper and continue cooking until the beans are tender and the soup has slightly thickened, about 5 minutes more. Discard bay leaf. Taste and adjust the seasonings. Ladle soup into warm bowls. Drizzle with extra-virgin olive oil. Serve hot along with fresh bread and feta cheese.

ARNI ME PATATES PSITO

Roasted Leg of Lamb with Potatoes
Serves 12

Greek Easter is a big celebration. Today, in the United States and all over Greece, Greeks celebrate Easter and cook whole lamb on spits. In this recipe, lamb is roasted in the oven along with potatoes which makes this dish not only taste so good, it makes the whole house smell good. This is also a great dish for a family get-together or any special occasion.

§ § § § §

1 5- to 6-pound bone-in leg of lamb, washed and trimmed of most fat
4 cloves garlic, slivered plus 2 whole cloves
Salt and freshly ground pepper to taste
1 tablespoon dried Greek oregano
1 fresh lemon
1/4 cup olive oil
4 large baking potatoes, peeled and cut into large wedges
2 cups vegetable stock
1 bay leaf

§ § § § §

Preheat oven to 425°F. With a boning knife, make a few small cuts deep enough to insert the garlic slivers into the lamb. Place the lamb in a roasting pan. Rub with salt, pepper, and oregano. Squeeze the lemon all over the lamb. Brush with olive oil. Place the lamb in the oven and roast, uncovered, for 20 minutes. Reduce the temperature to 375°F. Add the potatoes, stock, bay leaf, and garlic cloves to the roasting pan and continue roasting, basting often, for 1 hour and 10 minutes to 1 hour and 20 minutes (medium-rare will register 130°F to 140°F in the thickest part of the leg). Remove the lamb from the oven and transfer the meat to a cutting board. Let the meat rest for 15 minutes before carving. To serve, place the lamb on a serving platter along with the potatoes.

FAKES

Lentil Soup

Serves 5 to 6

This is the soup I ate so much of when I was young. A vegetarian soup that's simple to make with good fresh ingredients. If Greek or French lentils are not available, store bought lentils will do. Bowls of soup are usually drizzled with vinegar.

§ § § § § §

3 quarts cold water
1 cup finely chopped onions
1/4 cup finely chopped celery
1 cup brown lentils, preferably Greek or French, picked over and rinsed
3 tablespoons tomato paste
1 bay leaf
1clove garlic, peeled
1/2 teaspoon dried Greek oregano
1 tablespoons olive oil
Salt and pepper to taste
1/4 cup finely diced carrots
Red wine vinegar for drizzling.

§ § § § §

Place the water, onions and the celery in a large soup pot and bring to a boil over high heat. Reduce the heat to medium and boil, 10 minutes. Add the beans, tomato paste, bay leaf, garlic and oregano and cook for approximately 45 minutes, or until the lentils are just tender. Add the olive oil, salt, pepper, and the carrots and cook 5 minutes more. Discard bay leaf. Taste for seasonings. Serve warm accompanied by feta cheese and warm bread.

RATHIKIA ME LATHI KAI LEMONI

Boiled Dandelion Greens with Olive Oil and Lemon
Serves 2 to 4

Fresh boiled dandelion greens are a staple part of the cuisine. In Greece, Greek women go out to the fields and pick dandelion greens that grow wild. These greens are delicious and healthy. Generously season the dandelions with extra-virgin olive oil and lemon. Serve them along with your favorite fish or meat dish or as a light vegetarian lunch along with feta cheese and olives. You can find dandelion greens at most grocery stores or farmer's markets, but if you cannot find dandelions, substitute Swiss chard or broccoli rabe.

§§§§§§

1 bunch, about 1 pound, fresh dandelion greens, (Swiss chard or broccoli rabe) rinsed and picked over
1/2 teaspoon salt
1/2 to 1 whole lemon
1/4 cup extra-virgin olive oil

§§§§§§

Bring a large pot of salted water to a boil over high heat. Using tongs, add the greens to the pot. Simmer uncovered, and cook just until they are tender, about 5 to 10 minutes. Drain the dandelions and transfer to a serving bowl. Squeeze the lemon over the greens and drizzle with extra-virgin olive oil. Serve room temperature, accompanied with plenty of fresh bread for soaking up the juices.

Note: Swiss chard and broccoli rabe are tender greens and do not require as much cooking time.

KOKINAGOULIA

Boiled Beets Seasoned with Olive Oil and Garlic

Serves 2 to 4

These beets are best served warm along with the tender leaves in an olive oil vinaigrette with garlic. Serve them alone with fresh warm bread, feta cheese and olives or along with your favorite meal.

§ § § § § §

1 bunch fresh beets
1/4 cup extra-virgin olive oil
2 tablespoons of red wine vinegar
2 garlic cloves, coarsely chopped
Salt and pepper

§ § § § § §

Using a sharp knife, separate the beets from the leaves. Rinse and drain them in a colander. Place the beets in a large sauce pot and fill with water to cover. Bring the pot to a boil over high heat, and then reduce the heat to medium. Cook until the beets can be easily pierced with a fork, about 30 minutes. Remove the beets with a slotted spoon and set aside to cool. In the same pot, add more water if needed, then place the leaves and boil 5 minutes, or until tender when tested with a fork. Drain the greens and coarsely chop them. Peel and thinly slice the beets. Place the beets together with the beet leaves in a large serving bowl. In a small bowl, whisk together the olive oil, vinegar, garlic, salt and pepper. Pour the dressing over the beets and toss gently to mix. Place the beets in a serving bowl and enjoy.

IMAM BAILDI

Eggplant Simmered in a Tomato Sauce with Garlic and Olive Oil
Serves 4 to 6

There are many Greek dishes made with lots of olive oil. These dishes are known as oily dishes or ladthera. In this recipe, baby eggplants are tenderly simmered in a rich tomato sauce oozing with olive oil. This is best served room temperature as a mezé or appetizer, accompanied by warm bread or pita wedges.

§ § § § §

1 pound baby eggplants, (Italian, Chinese or Japanese) rinsed, and patted dry very well
15 whole garlic cloves
Approximately 1 cup olive oil for frying
1 large onion, cut in half and thinly sliced
1/2 cup tomato paste

2 cups vegetable stock
1 bay leaf
1 cinnamon stick
Salt and pepper to taste
Extra virgin olive oil for garnish

§ § § § §

Cut off the stems of the eggplants. Make a small cut in each eggplant and insert a garlic clove. Pour olive oil to 1 inch in a large frying pan. Heat until hot, but not smoking. Carefully add the eggplants, as many as will fit without overcrowding and sauté, until lightly golden and soft all over, about 4 to 5 minutes. Remove the eggplants with a slotted spoon and transfer them to a bowl. Continue with another batch adding more oil if needed, until all the eggplants are cooked. In the same pan, add the onions and any remaining garlic cloves and sauté until soft and translucent, about 5 minutes. Add the tomato paste, stock and stir to let the flavors blend. Add the bay leaf, cinnamon stick, salt and pepper. Taste for seasonings. Simmer and cook for 20 minutes, or until the sauce has slightly thickened. Remove and discard the bay leaf and cinnamon stick. Place in a serving bowl and drizzle with plenty of extra-virgin olive oil. Serve with warm bread.

SALTSA BÉCHAMEL

Béchamel Sauce
Makes about 2 cups

Béchamel Sauce is a white sauce and one of the mother sauces of French cuisine. It is the sauce used for moussaka and pastitsio. Italians use this in some lasagna recipes. A properly prepared bechamel should be a smooth and velvety consistency. Spoon it over cooked asparagus or broccoli, or over your favorite chicken Parmesan or meat dish and bake it in the oven until golden and bubbly or use it as the cream sauce for creamed chipped beef on toast.

§ § § § § §

2 cups whole milk
4 tablespoons clarified butter
4 tablespoons cake flour
Pinch ground nutmeg
Pinch ground cumin
Pinch salt and white pepper

§ § § § § §

Scald the milk in a medium sauce pan over low heat, being careful not to boil over. In another medium sauce pan, melt the butter over low heat. Add the flour and stir with a wooden spoon to form a paste. Cook over medium heat, stirring often to avoid burning, until the mixture is frothy and bubbly, about 2 minutes. Gradually add the hot milk to the roux while stirring constantly with a whisk. Bring to a boil. Reduce the sauce to a simmer. Add the nutmeg, cumin, salt, and white pepper. Cook over medium-low heat, whisking frequently until the sauce has thickened, about 30 minutes. Use right away or cool and store in the refrigerator for up to 2 days.

HALVA

Farina Dessert

Serves 10 to 12

Sliced almonds and cinnamon accent this quick and easy stove-top dessert. Traditionally olive oil is used in this recipe but I prefer butter, which provides an equally delicious flavor.

§ § § § §

For the Syrup:

2 1/2 cups sugar

5 cups water

2 whole cloves

1 cinnamon stick

2 teaspoons lemon juice

1/2 pound (2 sticks) unsalted butter

2 cups farina

Sliced almonds for garnish (optional)

Cinnamon for garnish

§ § § § §

Combine the sugar, water, cloves and cinnamon stick in a medium sauce pot. Stir to dissolve the sugar. Bring to a boil. Add the lemon juice and simmer, 5 minutes. Carefully remove the pot from the heat. Melt the butter in a large skillet over medium-high heat. Add the farina and stir continuously with a wooden spoon, 10 minutes or until lightly browned and bubbly. Remove the skillet from the heat. Carefully add the syrup in a slow steady stream to the farina mixture while constantly stirring. Return the skillet to the stove. Simmer, constantly stirring, until all of the liquids have absorbed and the mixture has thickened, about 5 minutes more. Remove the skillet from the heat. Pour the mixture into a large mold or bunt pan. Set aside to cool. Invert the mold over a large plate. Sprinkle with almonds and cinnamon. Slice and serve warm or cooled.

MOUSSAKA

A Casserole of Eggplant, Potatoes, and Beef with Béchamel Sauce
Serves 8 to 12

  This is a signature dish at my restaurant. Moussaka is a casserole dish of thinly sliced eggplant, potatoes and beef layered with Béchamel Sauce. Traditionally moussaka is cut into large square serving pieces. Accompany with a Greek salad.

§ § § § § §

3 medium eggplants (about 2 1/2 pounds), ends trimmed and thinly sliced 1/4 inch thick lengthwise

2 teaspoons salt for soaking

4 medium baking potatoes, peeled and thinly sliced 1/4 inch thick

2 tablespoons olive oil, plus more for brushing

Salt and pepper to taste

1 cup finely chopped onions

2 teaspoons minced garlic

2 pounds lean ground beef or lamb

1/2 cup dry red wine

1/2 cup tomato paste

1 bay leaf

4 cups Béchamel Sauce (see page 30)

1/2 cup grated kefalotiri or Parmesan cheese

§ § § § § §

Line a baking sheet with parchment and set aside. Soak the eggplant slices in a large bowl of cold, salted water for 1/2 hour to remove the moisture and the bitterness. Drain on absorbent paper. Heat the grill or broiler. Lightly brush the eggplant and potato slices with olive oil and season with salt and pepper. Grill or broil the eggplant and potato slices on both sides until just tender.

Place the eggplant and potato slices on the prepared baking sheet. Heat 2 tablespoons of the olive oil in a large frying pan over medium-high heat. Add the onions and garlic and cook until soft, about 5 minutes. Add the beef or lamb and cook until no longer pink. Add the wine and cook until almost all of the liquid has absorbed. Add the tomato paste. Taste for seasonings. Stir to let the flavors blend. Add the bay leaf. Reduce the heat to low. Simmer for 20 minutes. Remove the pan from the heat and discard the bay leaf. Preheat the oven to 350°F. Using a 13- x 9- x 2-inch baking dish, place half of the potato slices evenly into the bottom of the dish. Place half of the eggplant slices. Spread half of the meat mixture on top. Repeat with the remaining potatoes and eggplant slices. Spread the remaining meat mixture on top. Ladle the Béchamel Sauce evenly on top. Sprinkle with the cheese. Place the pan in the oven and bake for 45 minutes, or until nicely browned. Remove the dish from the oven. Allow to cool up to 1 hour before cutting.

Note: Leftovers can be wrapped and stored in the refrigerated for up to 2 days.

Variation: For vegetarian moussaka, omit the beef or the lamb and substitute with the following: 5 medium zucchini, rinsed well of all the sandy grit, thinly sliced and grilled or broiled as above. 4 medium red or green bell peppers, or a mixture of both, roasted, peeled, and sliced. Alternate with the eggplant and potato slices and top with a béchamel sauce.

KEFTEDES

Meatballs

Serves approximately 10 (makes about 3 dozen)

When I was growing up, the first thing I learned how to make was keftedes. For this recipe, the flavorful mint added to these savory meatballs makes them taste absolutely unforgettable. These make great party appetizers fried or baked in the oven. Serve them on a tray along with frilly toothpicks and accompany with tzatziki sauce for dipping, or serve them along with feta cheese and olives. A cold meatball sandwich on white bread with mayonnaise is best. Store the leftovers in baggies in the refrigerator, the kids love to eat them as snacks.

§ § § § § §

1/2 cup flour for dredging
1 pound lean ground beef (chuck)
1 small onion, grated
1 teaspoon finely minced garlic
2 teaspoon freshly chopped mint
2 teaspoons finely chopped fresh flat leaf or curly parsley
1/2 teaspoon salt
1/4 teaspoon pepper
1/2 cup plain breadcrumbs
1/4 cup grated kefalotiri or Parmesan cheese
2 eggs, beaten
Olive oil for frying

§ § § § § §

Place the flour in a medium size bowl and set aside. Place the beef, onions, garlic, mint, parsley, salt, pepper, bread crumbs, cheese and eggs in a large bowl. Knead until well combined. Using about 1 tablespoon of the meat mixture at a time, roll into small balls. Dredge each meatball in the flour and shake to remove excess. Pour the oil into a large frying pan, enough so that the oil will come 1/3 to 1/2 up the side of the meatball. Heat the oil over medium heat until hot, but not smoking. Carefully add the meatballs, as many as will fit with not over-crowding. Fry the meatballs on one side until brown, about 5 minutes. Using tongs, turn and brown until cooked, about 5 minutes more. Remove the meat balls with a slotted spoon and place on absorbent paper to drain. Serve warm or cooled.

Note: To bake, place the keftedes on a baking tray and bake them at 350°F for approximately 25 to 30 minutes until brown on both sides.

Variation: You could also substitute ground lamb for beef, or a mixture of beef, pork, and veal.

PASTICCIO

Baked Pasta Casserole with Beef

Serves 8

This is one dish that typifies Greek comfort food. A hearty, satisfying casserole made with layers of pasta and meat sauce, and topped with béchamel sauce. Pour a Kefalonian Robolla with this inspiring dish.

§§§§§§

2 tablespoons olive oil

2 cups finely chopped onions

2 pounds lean ground beef or ground lamb

1/2 cup dry red wine

1 tablespoon finely chopped garlic

4 tablespoons tomato paste

Salt and pepper to taste

1 bay leaf

1 cinnamon stick

1 pound Greek pasticcio pasta (sold at Greek specialty stores) or buccatinni pasta

5 cups Béchamel Sauce (see page 30)

11/2 cups grated kefalotiri or Parmesan cheese

§§§§§§

Heat the oil in a large skillet or frying pan over medium-high heat. Add the onions and sauté until soft, about 5 minutes. Add the beef or lamb and cook until no longer pink. Add the wine and cook until almost all of the liquid has been absorbed. Add the garlic, tomato paste, salt, and pepper. Stir to let the flavors blend. Add the bay leaf and cinnamon stick. Reduce the heat to low.

Simmer, 20 minutes. Remove the pan from the heat. Discard the cinnamon stick and bay leaf. Bring a large pot of lightly salted water to a brisk boil and cook the pasta until al dente or firm. Drain the pasta in a colander. Transfer the pasta to a large bowl and toss with 1 cup of the béchamel sauce. Set aside. Preheat the oven to 350°F. Oil or butter a 13- by 9-inch baking pan or casserole dish. Add half of the pasta to the prepared dish. Add the meat and spread it into an even layer using a spatula. Add the remaining pasta in an even layer and spread with the remaining béchamel sauce. Sprinkle with grated cheese and bake for 40 minutes, or until golden and bubbly. Remove from oven and allow to cool. Cut in large squares and serve warm.

KOTOPITA

Chicken in Phyllo with Avgolemono Sauce
Serves 4

This savory chicken roll wrapped in flaky phyllo pastry is an ideal choice for a buffet table or a special dinner. Saltsa Avgolemono spooned over each serving for an elegant finish just before serving. It's perfect with rice.

§ § § § §

4 tablespoons butter

4 skinless/boneless chicken breast halves, about 2 pounds, rinsed and patted dry

Salt and pepper to taste

2 cups chicken stock or more (see page 129)

1/2 cup finely chopped onions

1 large leek, rinsed well of all the sandy soil, white and light green parts trimmed and thinly sliced

1/2 cup finely chopped celery

Pinch of nutmeg

1/2 cup diced carrots

2 eggs, beaten,

6 sheets commercial phyllo pastry, thawed according to the package instructions

1/2 pound butter, melted for brushing the phyllo,

1 cup Saltsa Avgolemo (see page 39)

§ § § § §

Rub 1 tablespoon of the butter in a large skillet. Season the chicken with salt and pepper. Place the chicken in the skillet. Add 1 cup of the stock, partially cover and bring to a gentle simmer, 15 minutes or until the chicken is tender. Remove the chicken from the skillet and set aside to cool. Chop the chicken into small pieces and set aside. Wipe the skillet clean. Place the remaining 3 tablespoons of butter in the skillet on medium-high heat until the butter melts. Add the onions, leeks, celery, nutmeg, salt and pepper and sauté until the vegetables are almost soft, 5 minutes. Add the remaining stock and carrots, and continue to sauté until the almost all the liquids evaporate, about 5 minutes more. Set aside to cool slightly. Combine the chicken with the vegetables. Add the eggs and stir together. Preheat the oven to 350°F. Line a 13- x 9-inch baking sheet with parchment. Brush and layer one sheet of phyllo at a time with melted butter keeping the remaining sheets covered with plastic wrap until all the sheets are used. Spread the chicken mixture over the phyllo, leaving a 1-inch border on all sides. Turn the phyllo in around the edges and brush with the melted butter. Fold the phyllo over the chicken, until the phyllo dough is one long roll. Carefully place the chicken roll on the prepared baking pan, seam side down. Score the top of the crust to make marks where you will cut once it is done baking. Brush the chicken roll with the remaining melted butter and bake for 30 minutes, or until golden. Remove the pan from the oven. Place a slice of chicken roll on each plate. Spoon the sauce over the chicken. Serve immediately accompanied by rice pilaf.

SALTSA AVGOLEMONO

Egg-Lemon Sauce

Makes 1 cup

This is the classic sauce of Greek cuisine. It is made by vigorously whisking eggs and lemon juice with hot chicken stock on top of a double boiler. A properly made Saltsa Avgolemono should be lemon-colored and smooth, not loose. It is similar to a hollandaise sauce. Spoon this sauce over chicken in phyllo, warm stuffed dolmades, steamed asparagus, rice pilaf, or your favorite dish.

§ § § § §

1 cup chicken stock
3 large eggs
1/4 cup lemon juice
Salt to taste

§ § § § §

Heat the stock in a medium sauce pan over medium-high heat. Whisk the eggs until frothy in a stainless steel bowl. Whisk in the lemon juice. Slowly add the stock into the mixture whisking briskly. Place the bowl over a double boiler over low heat. Whisk the mixture continuously for 10 minutes, or until the sauce has thickened, like a slightly thickened whipped cream. Add the salt. Remove the bowl from the heat. Serve warm spooned over your favorite dish.

3
Kefalonia

Livathos

From the deck of the Strintzis Ferry, the sight of the Greek island, Kefalonia, rises up before me like a welcoming friend. I first went there in 1976, to visit the village of Lourdas or Lourdata, my father's birthplace. It was a mystical experience for me, for I felt as if, somehow, I had been there before. Even though I must have sailed here dozens of times, it's a place I keep returning. The ferry boat ride offers an unparalleled travel experience. I always enjoy the comfortable voyage on these big luxurious ships. Elegant salons and café bars on board offer delicious toast-cheese sandwiches and Greek coffee. Kefalonia is a sun-caressed outpost of paradise set in the Ionian Sea. Every year, thousands of people come to visit. They go to enjoy the pristine white sands, and the clear, inviting waters of its seaside resorts and breathtaking vistas of neighboring islands. I am one of those annual visitors, but my trips are more than a holiday. For me, Kefalonia is a home away from home. My favorite place is the beautiful Livathos municipality, located in the southwestern part of the island. Hundreds of pastel-colored picturesque villages, many with names ending with–ata, such as Moussata, Vlachiata and

Simotata, sit perched amidst the sublime beauty of Mt. Aenos. Enchanting beaches down below offer unsurpassed views of the Ionian Sea and the neighboring island of Zankinthos. While there I had the chance to climb Mt. Aenos, its main mountain which is covered by a unique species of fir trees (*Abies Cephonessis*). The tall imposing fir tree was associated with Zeus, the father of gods and men, and on Mt. Aenos there was once a temple dedicated to him. From this, its highest peak, you can see almost all the neighboring islands. For a moment I could almost visualize Odysseus sailing the Ionian Sea on one of his fabled journeys to Ithaki. During my climb on Mt. Aenos, I was able to view the unique Pindos, a breed of wild horses that are said to be direct descendants of those brought there by Alexander the Great. What a truly amazing site. I've been visiting Kefalonia for so many years now; it's not just a trip, it's become a part of my life.

The Kefalonian kitchen is unique and offers delights, centuries in the making. There are many dishes made with the island's fruity olive oil, the wild mountain herbs, and the vegeta-

bles. Especially good are the vegetables that come from the sea-side gardens of Lourdas. Tavernas and restaurants offer many local specialties such as *Kefalonitiki kreatopita* (meat pie), *skordalia* (garlicky mashed potatoes) and *kotopoulo riganato* (chicken oreganato). There are many pasta dishes with Venetian influences from the past such as *pastistsada* (spicy beef with pasta) and *carbonara* (creamy pasta with Italian bacon) and fabulous Corfiot dishes from the neighboring island of Corfu, such as *bianco* (a white fish casserole) and *sofrito* (veal cooked in a savory garlic sauce). From a young age, I always enjoyed cooking and I hope you enjoy these Kefalonian recipes.

KOTOPOULO KREASATOS

Chicken Stewed in a Marsala Wine Sauce

Serves 4

There are many chicken-in-the-pot meals. Kreasatos, is a method of cooking with wine which gives this dish a warm and interesting flavor. If boiler onions are not readily available, use shallots or pearl onions.

§ § § § §

3 tablespoons olive oil

1 to 3 1/2 pound chicken, preferably organic, rinsed, patted dry and cut into serving pieces

1 pound small white boiler onions, peeled

4 garlic cloves, sliced

1 teaspoon red wine vinegar

1/2 cup sweet Marsala wine

1 cup tomato sauce

2 cups chicken stock

Sachet:1 bay leaf, 1 cinnamon stick, 4 allspice berries, 4 peppercorns placed into a piece of cheesecloth and tied with butchers twine

1 teaspoon salt

1/2 teaspoon white pepper

§ § § § §

Heat the oil in a large stewing pot over medium-high heat until hot. Add the chicken, browning well on all sides, about 5 to 8 minutes. Add the onions and the garlic and sauté until the garlic is aromatic and soft, about 1 to 2 minutes. Add the vinegar and steam off a minute or two. Add the wine, tomato sauce, and the stock, just enough to cover. Stir to blend. Add the sachet, salt and white pepper. Simmer and cook approximately 30 to 40 minutes, or until the chicken is tender and the sauce has slightly thickened. Taste and adjust the seasonings. Remove the pot from the heat. Discard the sachet. Place a portion of chicken on individual serving dishes. Serve accompanied by rice or pasta and spoon some of the sauce on top.

STRAPATSATHA

Eggs with Tomatoes and Feta Cheese

Serves 4

This recipe is a nice change to scrambled eggs. My father used to make this dish for breakfast for us when I was growing up. Little did I know then, that this recipe is unique to Kefalonia. The tomatoes are the main ingredient in this specialty. The addition of chopped green peppers or onions works well too. Serve for breakfast or a light lunch or meal.

§ § § § § §

1/4 cup olive oil
2 large tomatoes, grated
Pinch of salt and pepper
1 cup crumbled feta cheese
8 eggs, lightly beaten.

§ § § § § §

Heat the oil in a large skillet over medium-high heat. Add the tomatoes and cook until soft, about 5 minutes. Add the salt and pepper. Simmer over low heat, until the tomatoes become like a sauce, about 5 minutes more. Add the cheese and stir to blend. Add the eggs, stirring lightly to scramble. Cook until set but not dry. Carefully slide the eggs onto a serving plate. Serve warm accompanied by fried potatoes and toast.

RIGANATHA

Tomato and Crumbled Feta Cheese Rusks

Serves 4

Riganatha is unique to the Kefalonian cuisine. This is a quick and easy recipe similar to brushetta topped with tomatoes and feta cheese. It's a great way to use up dried or any leftover bread. Serve it as a snack or as a mezé or starter before your main course, or serve it along with a bowl of fassoulatha soup!

§ § § § §

4 slices dried bread or French baguette, cut into 1-inch thick slices
2 ripe plum tomatoes, diced
4 tablespoons extra-virgin olive oil
Pinch of salt and pepper
1 tablespoon red wine vinegar
1/2 cup crumbled feta cheese
2 teaspoons dried Greek oregano

§ § § § §

Very lightly sprinkle the stale bread with cold water to moisten the bread. Arrange the bread slices on a serving plate. Combine the diced tomatoes, olive oil, salt, pepper and vinegar in a medium bowl and stir. Spoon 1 tablespoon of tomato mixture on each slice of bread. Garnish with feta cheese. Sprinkle with oregano and serve.

PASTITSATHA

Pasta and Beef in a Tomato Wine Sauce

Serves 4

Pastitsatha is a specialty dish of the Ionian Islands and one of my favorite recipes. For this recipe, tender chunks of beef are simmered in a rich tomato sauce. Thick bucatini pasta is added towards the end of the cooking process. Complement this dish with a glass of Ano Kefkimi, a Corfiot red wine of Koulouris. Kali Orexi (Good Appetite).

§ § § § § §

1/4 cup olive oil

1 1/2 to 2 pounds boneless chuck roast, cut into 2 inch pieces

1 medium onion, coarsely chopped

3 garlic cloves, sliced

1 tablespoon red wine vinegar

1/2 cup sweet Marsala wine

2 cups tomato sauce

1/2 teaspoon dried marjoram

1/2 teaspoon dried thyme

2 tablespoons butter

1 teaspoon sugar

Sachet: 1 cinnamon stick, 1 bay leaf, 2 whole cloves placed in a piece of cheesecloth and tied with butchers twine

1/2 teaspoon salt

1/4 teaspoon pepper

3 1/2 cups vegetable stock

1/2 pound bucatini pasta or perciateli, cooked according to directions

Myzithra cheese or hard Italian ricotta salata for garnish

§ § § § § §

Heat the oil in a heavy pot on medium-high heat until hot. Add the beef and brown on all sides, 5 minutes. Add the onions and garlic to the pot and sauté for 5 minutes, or until soft. Add the vinegar and steam off. Add the wine, tomato sauce, marjoram, thyme, butter, sugar, sachet, salt, pepper and 2 cups of the stock, or enough to cover. Cover, reduce the heat and simmer for 1 hour and 45 minutes or until the beef is almost fork tender. Uncover the pot. Add the pasta to the pot. Add the remaining stock, adding more if necessary and cook uncovered, stirring the pasta occasionally until the pasta is al dente and the sauce has thickened. Remove the pot from the heat. Discard the sachet. Taste for seasonings. Place the pastitsada in a large pretty serving bowl. Sprinkle with shavings of myzithra cheese and serve warm.

SKORDALIA

Garlicky Mashed Potatoes

Serves 4

The secret to these garlicky potatoes is to pound them into a creamy paste. The results are excellent. Traditionally in Greece, these potatoes are pounded in a large mortar with pestle. Since many of us are not equipped with these in our kitchens, a potato masher will do fine. Serve accompanied by fried bakaliaros and boiled beets.

§ § § § § §

10 garlic cloves, peeled
1 cup plus 4 tablespoons extra virgin olive oil
1/2 cup plus 1 tablespoon freshly squeezed lemon juice
4 large russet potatoes, washed, peeled and quartered
Salt to taste
1/2 to 1 cup warm fish stock (see page 125), as needed
Extra-virgin olive oil for drizzling

§ § § § § §

Place the garlic, 4 tablespoons of the olive oil and 1 tablespoon lemon juice in a food processor and pulverize into a smooth paste. Set aside. Place the potatoes in a medium pot. Cover with salted water and bring to a boil. Simmer and cook until the potatoes are tender, but not overcooked, about 10 minutes Drain them well in a colander. In a large bowl, while the potatoes are still hot, mash the potatoes one at a time. Add the garlic mixture, salt, the remaining cup of olive oil, and the remaining lemon juice alternately. Add the fish stock, a little bit at a time, adding more if needed to make a creamy mixture. Taste for seasonings. Drizzle with extra virgin olive oil and serve room temperature.

BIANCO

White Fish Casserole

Serves 4

This is a classic Corfiot dish from the neighboring Island of Corfu. A white fish casserole combines the flavors of garlic, leeks, potatoes, lemon, and olive oil. A good Corfiot wine would be Santa Domenica from kakotrygis grapes.

§ § § § § §

4 cups fish stock, or vegetable stock

4 tablespoons olive oil

2 large leeks, rinsed well and thinly sliced

1 small carrot, peeled and cut into thin julienne sticks

10 garlic cloves, thinly sliced

2 sun dried tomatoes, thinly sliced

Juice of 2 fresh lemons

2 teaspoons dried Greek oregano

Salt and white pepper to taste

4 small red or white potatoes, peeled, and sliced into thin rounds

4 (6- to 8-ounce) pieces (1 1/2 to 2 pounds) of fresh filet of cod, halibut, or haddock,

2 tablespoons chopped fresh flat leaf or curly parsley

§ § § § § §

Heat the stock in a large casserole pot over medium-high heat. Add the olive oil, leeks, carrots, garlic, tomatoes, lemon juice, oregano, salt and pepper. Simmer for approximately 5 minutes. Add the potatoes and continue cooking 5 minutes more, or until the potatoes are just about tender. Place the fish in the pan over the potatoes. Simmer approximately10 minutes, until the fish is just cooked through and the liquid is reduced and sauce like. Taste and adjust the seasonings. Remove the pan from the heat. Divide the fish among four serving dishes. Ladle the sauce over the fish. Sprinkle with chopped parsley and serve right away.

KEFALONITIKI KREATOPITA TSI THIAS MARINAS

Aunt Marina's Kefalonian Meat Pie

Serves 6

This is a traditional recipe hailing from Kefalonia. This recipe is from my Aunt Marina who lives in the village of Kerames, Kefalonia. It is also the village where my Yiayia Anezina was born. In this incredible meat pie, tiny pieces of beef with rice and fragrant spices are enveloped in a phyllo pastry that is rich with fragrant olive oil and wine. Cut in large square pieces. Serve warm and cork open a bottle of light and savory Ktima Calliga from Inoexagoyiki.

§ § § § §

For the Phyllo:

3 to 3 1/2 cups flour

1 cup warm water

1 cup olive oil

1 cup dry white wine

1 teaspoon salt

Olive oil for brushing the phyllo

For the Filling:

11/2 pounds chuck stewing beef, cut into tiny pieces

1/2 cup olive oil

1 large onion, finely chopped

2 large ripe tomatoes, chopped

3 tablespoons tomato paste

3 garlic cloves, chopped

1/3 cup chopped parsley

1/2 teaspoon cinnamon

Salt and pepper to taste

2 cups vegetable stock

1 cup rice

§ § § § §

Make the Phyllo: Grease a 13- by 9- by 2-inch baking pan and set aside. Place the flour in a large mixing bowl. Make a well in the center. Add the warm water, olive oil, wine and salt. Work the flour into the liquid with your hands, until the dough begins to form. Turn the dough out to a pastry board dusted with flour. Knead the dough for about 20 minutes, until the dough is soft and elastic. Cover the dough with a clean kitchen cloth and place it in a warm place to rest, 1 hour.

Make the Filling: Place the beef in a large pot and add water just to cover. Bring to a boil, cook for 1 minute. Remove the pot from the heat and drain in a colander. Heat the oil in a large frying pan over medium-high heat. Add the beef cubes and brown all over, about 10 minutes. Add the onions and cook until soft, 5 minutes. Add the tomatoes, tomato paste, garlic, parsley, cinnamon, salt, pepper and stock. Reduce the heat and simmer, 5 minutes. Add the rice and stir. Taste for seasonings. Remove the pan from the stove. Place the filling in a bowl and set aside to cool. Preheat the oven to 350°F. Turn the dough out onto a lightly floured surface and knead for 10 minutes. Divide the dough in half, one slightly larger than the other. With a rolling pin, roll and stretch the larger half of the dough out to a thickness of 1/3 of an inch. Lay the dough in the baking pan allowing for the dough to overlap along the edges of the pan by about 1 inch. Spread the filling evenly into the pan. Repeat the rolling process for the remaining piece of dough and place the dough evenly over the top of the filling. Roll and pinch in the edges to seal the crust. Brush all of the pastry with oil. Prick the pie all over with a fork. Place the pie in the oven and bake for 45 minutes, or until lightly golden. Remove the pie from the oven and let it cool to room temperature.

SPAGHETTO NAPOLITAN

Spaghetti with Tomato Sauce

Serves 6 to 8

There are many Venetian-inspired pasta dishes served in many restaurants in Kefalonia. This specialty for spaghetto napolitan is an Italian classic. Serve this rich meatless tomato sauce and pasta dish along with a Greek salad.

§ § § § §

For the Sauce: (makes about 3 cups)

1/4 cup olive oil

2 tablespoons butter

2 pounds fresh plum tomatoes, diced (*see note*) or 2 cups canned diced or crushed tomatoes with their juices

1 cup warm vegetable stock

1/2 of one small onion

3 to 4 garlic cloves, crushed

1 teaspoon dried Greek oregano

1 teaspoon sugar

Salt and pepper to taste

1 small carrot, peeled and cut in half

1 bay leaf

1 tablespoon tomato paste

1/4 cup red wine

For the Pasta:

1 pound ribbon pasta, penne, rigatoni or other tubular pasta

2 tablespoons olive oil

1 tablespoon butter

1 garlic clove, minced

Kefalotiri for garnish (optional)

§ § § § §

Make the Sauce: Heat the oil and the butter in a large sauce pot over medium-high heat. Add the tomatoes and cook until the tomatoes begin to soften, about 5 minutes. Add the stock, onion, garlic, oregano, sugar, salt, pepper, carrot and bay leaf. Add the tomato paste and wine and stir with a wooden spoon until the mixture is well blended. Reduce the heat to low and simmer for 1 hour, or until the sauce thickens. Remove the bay leaf, onion, and carrot.

Make the Pasta: Bring a large pot of salted water to a brisk boil and cook the pasta until al dente or firm. Drain the pasta. Wipe the pot clean. Heat the olive oil and the butter in the same pot. Add the garlic and sauté until fragrant but not brown, about 1 minute. Return the pasta to the pot. Toss over medium heat to combine, about 2 minutes. Remove the pot from the heat. Place the pasta in a large serving bowl. Ladle the sauce over the pasta. Sprinkle with kefalotiri cheese and serve right away.

Note: If you are using fresh tomatoes: make a small cut through the skin on the bottom of each tomato. Blanch the tomatoes in boiling water for 30 to 60 seconds. Place the tomatoes in a cool ice bath. Core and peel the tomatoes. Cut the tomatoes in half and squeeze out the seeds and the juices. Pulse or dice them in a food processor.

KOTOPOULO RIGANNATO

Roasted Chicken with Oregano

Serves 4

I always use organic chickens because I find they are more flavorful. For this recipe, the fragrant Greek oregano gives this dish a superb flavor. You can substitute rice or pasta instead of the potatoes, or complement this dish by adding a box of frozen peas and carrots toward the end of the cooking. This makes a great family dinner.

§ § § § §

1 organic chicken (about 3 1/2 pounds), rinsed, patted dried, and most of the skin removed
Juice of one whole lemon
Salt and pepper to taste
1/2 cup olive oil
5 cloves garlic, sliced
2 tablespoons dried Greek oregano
1 bay leaf
2 cups chicken or vegetable stock
6 baking potatoes, peeled and quartered

§ § § § §

Preheat oven to 375°F. Place chicken in a large roasting pan. Pour the lemon over chicken. Sprinkle with salt and pepper. Drizzle with olive oil. Add garlic, oregano and the bay leaf. Pour the stock into the pan. Roast uncovered, for 30 minutes, basting every 15 minutes. Add the potatoes and continue roasting for 30 minutes more or until the chicken is tender and a thermometer reads 170°F when inserted into the thigh. Remove the pan from the oven. Arrange the chicken and potatoes all around on a platter. Pour some of the pan juices over the chicken and potatoes. Serve accompanied by warm bread for soaking up the juices.

SOFRITO

Veal Sofrito

Serves 4

This traditional Corfiot dish is the perfect Sunday meal. The vinegar, garlic, and parsley added to the pan create a savory sauce. Typically this dish is usually served accompanied by mashed potatoes or rice. Fingerling potatoes would go great.

§ § § § § §

4 veal scallops, pounded (about 6 ounces) each
Pinch of salt, pepper
Flour for dredging
1/2 cup olive oil
4 to 5 garlic cloves, slivered
1/3 cup red wine vinegar
1/3 cup chopped fresh flat leaf or curly parsley
1 tablespoon butter

§ § § § § §

Season the veal scallops with salt and pepper. Lightly dredge in flour and shake off excess. Heat the oil in a large sauté pan over medium-high heat until hot, but not smoking. Add the veal scallops and sauté on each side for approximately 2 to 3 minutes. Remove the veal scallops to a warm platter. Add the garlic to the pan and sauté. Deglaze the pan with the vinegar. Add the parsley and the butter. Return the veal to the sauce. Taste for seasonings. Place the veal on to warm plates or a serving platter. Spoon the sauce over the veal. Serve right away.

MAKARONIA BOLOGNESE

Serves 4

Makaronia Bolognese is one of my favorite pasta dishes. Bolognese is a meat-based sauce for pasta originating in Bologna, Italy. In Kefalonia, there are many Italian inspired pasta dishes from the once Venetian rule. If you have a crock pot, make the sauce early in the day to have it ready just in time for dinner.

§ § § § §

For the Sauce:

3 tablespoons olive oil

1 tablespoon butter

1/2 cup finely chopped onions

1/4 cup finely chopped celery

1 pound lean ground beef, chuck

1/2 cup dry red wine

1 pound fresh plum tomatoes, diced (see page 56) or 1 1/2 cups canned crushed tomatoes

1 cup vegetable stock

1/4 cup finely diced carrots

1 bay leaf

4 garlic cloves, minced

Salt and pepper to taste

1 teaspoon dried Greek oregano

1 teaspoon sugar

For the Pasta:

1/2 pound tagliatelle or pappardelle pasta

Freshly grated kefalotiri cheese or Parmesan for garnish

§ § § § §

Make the Sauce: Heat the oil and the butter in a large sauté pan over medium-high heat until hot. Add the onions and celery and sauté until tender, about 5 minutes. Add the beef and cook until no pink remains. Add the wine and cook until almost all the juices have evaporated. Stir in the tomatoes and stock. Add the carrots, bay leaf, garlic, salt, pepper, oregano, and sugar. Stir to blend the flavors. Simmer, uncovered over medium-low heat and cook about 1 hour, or until the sauce has thickened.

Make the Pasta: While the sauce is cooking, bring a large pot of salted water to a brisk boil and cook the pasta, stirring until al dente, or firm. Drain the pasta and return it to the pot. Remove the bay leaf from the sauce. Adjust the seasonings. Combine the sauce and pasta. Place the pasta in a large pasta bowl. Sprinkle with the cheese and serve hot along with a Greek salad.

CARBONARA

Pasta Carbonara

Serves 6

Although pasta carbonara is a classic Italian dish, it is a real favorite in Kefalonia. Pietros' in Argostoli serves a wonderful carbonara. This is a rich and creamy pasta dish made with Italian pancetta, eggs, and cheese. The addition of peas adds texture and color. This dish is similar to fettuccini alfredo. Serve this dish as soon as it is prepared. A chilled glass of limoncello is the perfect aperitif for this meal.

§ § § § §

1 pound fettuccine or thick spaghetti pasta

1 tablespoon butter

4 ounces pancetta, chopped into small pieces

1 garlic cloves, minced

1/2 cup heavy cream

6 ounces Parmesan cheese

1 cup frozen peas

Salt and white pepper to taste

2 egg yolks, beaten

§ § § § §

Make the Pasta: Bring a large pot of salted water to a brisk boil and cook the pasta until al dente or firm. Drain the pasta and set aside.

Make the Carbonara: Melt the butter in a large sauté pan over medium-high heat. Add the pancetta and cook until just beginning to crisp. Add the garlic and sauté, but not brown, 1 minute. Add the pasta to the pan and toss to heat completely. Add the heavy cream and bring to a simmer. Add the Parmesan, peas, salt and pepper and toss. Add the egg yolks to the pot and quickly stir until well coated and to thicken the sauce. Remove the pot from the heat and serve right away.

HORIATIKI SALATA

Village Salad

Serves 2 to 4

The warm summer months and the wonderfully mild climate of Greece allow the fruits and vegetables, especially the tomatoes grown there to burst with flavor. For this salad you will need perfectly ripe tomatoes. Toss the salad altogether and serve it in a pretty clear-glass salad bowl. The flavorful Greek oregano brings it altogether.

§ § § § § §

2 large ripe tomatoes, cut into chunky wedges

2 medium cucumbers, preferably seedless, peeled and sliced into chunky rounds

1 small green bell pepper, cored, seeded, and cut into thin rings

1 small red onion, halved and thinly sliced

8 Kalamata olives

1/2 pound crumbled feta cheese

4 Pepperochini peppers

Greek Salad Dressing (see page 133)

1 teaspoon dried Greek oregano

§ § § § § §

Place the tomatoes, cucumbers, peppers, onions, olives, cheese, and pepperochini in a large salad bowl. Drizzle with 2 to 3 tablespoons of the Greek salad dressing and toss gently to mix. Serve alone or accompanied by your favorite meal.

4
Family

I never thought I would write a book about myself. My life has been long and interesting. My *Nono* (Godfather) often told me that I never ceased to amaze him and my friends believe my story will serve as an inspiration to others who have faced the similar hardships. Friends say I should have been on "Oprah." I've learned about family values and the importance of family from my parents. Being divorced, I was both a mother and a father to my children. I worked hard to get where I am today. I became jack-of-all trades and took on various jobs. I did everything I possibly could to make ends meet. Life was not easy but, being a stubborn Greek lady, I survived. I became a strong and independent person. Throughout all of this, I always managed to have dinner on the table for my family every night. I've succeeded in raising a wonderful family. My daughter Elena, and my sons, Theo and Tony, have stuck by me. They are my best cheerleaders and I love them dearly. Food plays an important role in Greek life. It keeps the family together. On holidays and special occasions we look forward to cooking and celebrating together, with both family and friends. In many ways, we still celebrate just like the ancient Greeks did at symposiums, telling stories in the company of food and wine. I've collected recipes for as long as I can remember, and I still have my collections of Bon Appetité magazines piled high, with issues dating back to the 1980s. I love to go to the market, look at the wonderfully fresh produce, and dream up fantastic dishes using what I've found. The best meals were made from the most inexpensive ingredients. I call these Greek soul-satisfying comfort foods. As soon as I got my life back in order after my divorce, I began taking annual vacations to Greece with the kids. Spending time there became almost an addiction, and we traveled there almost every summer. It was at this time I realized my strong love for the country that is my heritage and developed a passion for its cuisine, almost to the point of obsession. It was something we looked forward to and talked about all year.

PATATES LATHORIGANO

Roasted Potatoes with Olive Oil, Oregano and Lemon
Serves 6

These roasted Greek potatoes are usually served accompanied by lamb, fish, or chicken. I like to bake them until they are crisp and browned all over, which makes them taste so good.

§ § § § §

3 large russet potatoes, peeled and quartered
1/2 cup olive oil
Juice of 1 whole lemon
Salt and pepper to taste
2 teaspoons dried Greek oregano

§ § § § §

Place the potatoes in a medium saucepan filled with enough cold water to cover them. Bring to a boil over high heat. Cook until just firm, about 2 to 3 minutes. Drain and cool under cold running water. Place the potatoes in a single layer in a baking dish. Preheat oven to 425˚F. In a small bowl, whisk together the olive oil, lemon juice, salt, pepper and oregano. Pour the olive oil mixture all over the potatoes. Place the baking sheet in the oven and bake for 15 minutes or until the potatoes are golden brown. Serve hot.

HILOPITES ME MYZITHRA

Pasta Squares with Myzithra Cheese

Serves 4

Hilopites are tiny, square, fun-shaped pasta and a culinary treasure. The best come from the Peloponnese, where the locals make them from scratch. My children grew up on these when they were young. When I visit Greece, I always bring some back home. These are best served alone with butter and plenty of myzithra cheese or as a side dish drizzled with tomato sauce, or alongside chicken or meat.

§ § § § §

2 cups hilopites pasta, sold at Greek specialty shops
4 tablespoons butter
Approximately 1 cup grated myzithra cheese or Italian hard ricotta salata

§ § § § §

Bring a large pot of lightly salted water to a brisk boil and cook the pasta until al dente. Drain the pasta. Melt the butter in the same pot. Return the pasta to the pot. Toss over medium heat to combine, about 2 minutes. Remove the pot from the heat. Place the pasta in individual pasta dishes. Garnish with plenty of grated myzithra cheese and serve immediately while hot.

KOTOPOULO ME HILOPITES TIS KATSAROLAS

Chicken in the Pot with Pasta Squares

Serves 4

This is another great chicken in-the-pot meal. Tiny pasta squares called *hilopites,* make this dish so unique. Hilopites can be found at Greek grocery stores, but if they are not available, substitute orzo pasta. Serve with plenty of shavings of myzithra cheese.

§ § § § §

4 tablespoons olive oil

1 chicken (about 3 1/2 pounds), preferably organic, most of the skin removed, rinsed, patted dried and cut into serving pieces

1 large onion, chopped

2 garlic cloves, slivered

1 cup crushed tomatoes

1/2 cup tomato sauce

4 cups chicken stock

2 tablespoons butter

1 teaspoon salt

Sachet: 1 bay leaf, 4 allspice berries, 3 peppercorns, tied in a piece of cheesecloth with butchers twine

2 cups hilopites pasta—found at Greek specialty shops

Grated myzithra cheese or Italian hard ricotta salata for garnish

§ § § § § §

Heat the oil in a large stewing pot over medium-high heat until hot. Add the chicken and sear on all sides, about 10 minutes. Add the onions and garlic and sauté until they are translucent. Add the crushed tomatoes, tomato sauce, and 2 cups of the stock, butter, and salt and stir to blend. Add the sachet to the pot. Simmer and cook for about 30 minutes covered, until the chicken is almost tender. Add the pasta and 2 cups of the remaining stock and cook, uncovered, until the chicken is tender and the pasta is cooked, about 10 to 12 minutes. Remove the sachet. Place a portion of chicken with some of the pasta on individual serving dishes. Garnish with plenty of grated myzithra cheese and serve hot.

KOTA ATZEM PILAFI

Chicken in the Pot with Rice

Serves 4

Atzem is a method of cooking along with rice. In Greece, these hearty stove-top meals are made for large families. They are usually prepared early in the day, and kept warm to have just in time for dinner.

§ § § § §

4 tablespoons olive oil

1 2 1/2 to 3 pound chicken, washed, most of the skin removed and cut into serving pieces

1 cup chopped onions

3 garlic cloves, crushed

1 cup tomato sauce

1 teaspoon salt

1/2 teaspoon pepper

2 tablespoons butter

2 1/2 cups chicken stock plus more

1 bay leaf

1 cup white rice

§ § § § §

Heat the oil in a large stewing pot over medium-high heat until hot. Add the chicken and brown until golden on all sides, about 10 minutes. Add the onions and garlic, cook until soft. Add the tomato sauce, salt, pepper, butter, stock and the bay leaf. Simmer and cook for approximately 30 minutes covered, until the chicken is almost tender. Add the rice and cook until the chicken is tender and the rice is cooked, about 20 minutes more. Remove the pot from heat. Discard the bay leaf. Taste to adjust the seasonings. Place a portion of chicken and rice onto individual plates and serve accompanied by a Greek salad.

RIZI ME FITHE KAI KOUKOUNARIA

Rice with Noodles and Pine Nuts

Serves 4 to 6

This appetizing pilaf is interesting enough to serve on its own. The added pine nuts make a nice indulgent touch. Serve it as a side dish or accompanied by your favorite dish.

§ § § § § §

2 tablespoons butter
1/2 cup pine nuts
1 cup vermicelli
1 cup white rice
2 cups chicken stock
1 teaspoon salt

§ § § § § §

Melt the butter in a large skillet over medium heat. Add the pine nuts and vermicelli. Sauté gently until golden brown, about 3 minutes. Add the rice and stir to coat. Add the stock and the salt. Bring to a boil. Simmer and cook, covered, without stirring for 15 minutes, or until the rice is almost tender. Remove the pan from the heat and let it rest a few minutes. Fluff with a fork and serve immediately.

Note: You can add chopped scallions or currents to this dish.

SPANAKORIZO

Spinach and Rice

Serves 4

What I remember most about growing up was the delicious meatless meals we made with fresh vegetables smothered in a fruity olive oil. This is one of the simplest stove-top recipes. A delicious combination of spinach and rice simmered in a delicate tomato sauce. Serve as a side dish along with meat, poultry, or fish, or double the recipe for a main vegetarian meal.

§ § § § §

3 tablespoons olive oil

1/2 cup finely chopped onions

2 teaspoons minced garlic

2 cups vegetable stock

1 cup tomato sauce

1 cup white rice

Salt and pepper to taste

1 10-ounce bag spinach, rinsed

§ § § § §

Heat the oil in a large saucepan over medium heat. Add the onions and garlic and sauté until soft, about 5 minutes. Add the stock, tomato sauce, rice, salt, and pepper and stir to blend. Add the spinach. Cover, reduce the heat to simmer and cook about 15 to 20 minutes. Serve warm.

STIFATHO

Stewed Beef with Sweet Onions

Serves 4

This is an intensely flavorful stew that is slowly cooked in wine with sweet onions. It's absolutely delicious to serve on a winter evening. Serve accompanied by rice.

§ § § § § §

3 tablespoons olive oil

2 pounds boneless beef chuck, cut into 1- to 2-inch pieces

4 garlic cloves, sliced

1 teaspoon red wine vinegar

1/2 cup sweet Marsala wine

2 cups vegetable stock

1 cup tomato sauce

1 teaspoon sugar

Sachet: 1 bay leaf, 1 cinnamon stick, 4 allspice berries, 4 peppercorns, placed into a piece of cheesecloth and tied with butchers twine

1 teaspoon salt

1/4 teaspoon pepper

1 pound small white boiler onions, peeled shallots, or pearl onions

§ § § § § §

Heat the oil in a large stewing pot over medium-high heat. Add the meat and cook until browned on all sides, about 10 minutes. Add the garlic and cook just until aromatic. Add the vinegar and steam off a minute. Add the wine and stock. Add the tomato sauce, sugar, sachet, salt, and pepper and stir to blend. Cover, simmer for 1 hour. Add the onions and continue cooking until the beef is fork tender and sauce has slightly thickened, about 1 more hour. Remove sachet. Place a portion of rice on each serving dish. Spoon some of the stifatho over top. Serve immediately.

FASOULAKIA ME PATATES YAHNI

Stewed Green Beans and Potatoes in a Tomato Sauce

Serves 4

Yahni is a method of stewing with tomatoes and onions, similar to a ragout. This is a hearty vegetarian dish, and one that my kids always enjoyed when they were young. It's simple and quick, made with a few, staple ingredients. Make this in the crock pot. If you're pressed for time, buy frozen green beans, they work well, too.

§ § § § § §

3/4 cup olive oil

2 cups chopped onions

3 garlic cloves, sliced

1 pound fresh green beans, ends snapped off

1 cup tomato sauce or chopped fresh tomatoes

2 cups vegetable stock

4 white potatoes, peeled and cut into wedges

1/2 teaspoon salt

1/4 teaspoon pepper

1 bay leaf

§ § § § § §

Heat the oil in a large stewing pot over medium-high heat. Add the onions and garlic and sauté until soft, about 5 minutes. Add the green beans and sauté about 5 minutes. Add tomato sauce, stock, potatoes, salt, and pepper and stir to blend. Add the bay leaf. Cover and simmer 45 minutes, or until the beans and potatoes are tender and sauce has thickened. Remove the bay leaf. Serve warm accompanied by plenty of warm bread for soaking up the juices.

PRASORIZO

Braised Leeks with Rice

Serves 4

You wouldn't believe the incredible vegetarian meals that you can make with just a few ingredients. Not only are they healthy, but they are incredibly delicious and simple to make. If you like rice, you'll be sure to love this inspiring dish of rice and braised leeks. Serve it as a side dish along with your favorite meat, fish, or chicken.

§ § § § §

4 tablespoons olive oil

1 bunch leeks (about 1 1/2 pounds), rinsed well of all the sandy soil, white and light green parts sliced into thin rounds

Juice of 1 lemon

2 cups vegetable stock

Salt and pepper to taste

1 cup rice

§ § § § §

Heat the oil in a large sauce pan over medium-high heat. Add the leeks and sauté until soft without browning, about 8 minutes. Add the lemon, stock, salt, pepper, and rice and stir to blend. Cover, reduce the heat to simmer, and cook 15 to 20 minutes. Serve warm.

AVGOLEMONO SOUPA

Egg-Lemon Soup

Serves 8

This is a very flavorful chicken soup with lots of lemon. In this recipe, the soup is carefully thickened on its own without any starches or flour, almost reminding you of a creamed soup. You can make this soup a day in advance without the pasta to keep it fresh. Make the pasta and add it to the soup when ready to serve.

§ § § § § §

1 chicken (about 3 pounds), preferably organic, rinsed and partially skinned

2 quarts cold water

1 small onion, peeled and left whole

1 small carrot, peeled and cut into 2 to 3 pieces

1 celery rib cut in 2 to 3 pieces

1 bay leaf

1 cup orzo pasta

Salt and white pepper to taste

4 large eggs

Juice of 1 to 2 lemons

Fresh flat leaf or curly parsley, chopped for garnish

§ § § § § §

Place the chicken and the water in a large stock pot. Bring to a boil. Add the onion, carrot, celery, and bay leaf. Reduce the heat to low and cook, skimming the foam that forms, for 1 hour, or until the chicken is falling from the bones. Remove the pot from the heat. Place the chicken in a large bowl and set aside to cool. Strain the stock. Remove the vegetables. Place the stock in a large soup pot and bring to a boil. Add the pasta, salt and pepper. Reduce the heat and simmer 10 minutes, or until the orzo is just tender. Whisk the eggs until frothy in a stainless steel bowl. Slowly pour in the lemon juice. Whisking constantly, slowly pour 2 cups of the hot stock into the egg-lemon mixture. Continuing to whisk, slowly pour this egg mixture back into the remaining stock. Simmer on very low heat, and cook, whisking constantly for 10 minutes or until the soup has thickened. Cut or pull the meat from the chicken. Add to the soup. Taste and adjust the seasonings adding more lemon if needed. Ladle into soup bowls. Garnish with parsley and serve hot along with a Greek salad.

5
Proinos Kafes
Morning Coffee

It was in the early 90s that I started taking frequent trips to Greece with the kids. We usually stayed in Glyfada at the Johns Hotel before heading to our family home in Kefalonia. One of my favorite memories of Greece is the continental breakfast that is served at many hotels. Breakfast usually consists of orange juice, coffee and toast rusks with jam, hard boiled eggs, sliced pound cake and yogurt. It was the same each and every time I visited. Many times, I traveled to Greece by myself to take care of the family land inheritance. Sometimes I would stay in Athens at the boutique St. George Lycabettus Hotel, located in chic Kolonaki. I always enjoyed having the breakfast buffet here on the breakfast room floor, the "Le Grand Balcon," which offers stunning panoramic views of the city and the Sarconic Gulf. Greeks have a passion for coffee almost to the point of obsession. It's not unusual to see coffee delivered down the tiny streets and alleyways on swinging no-spill trays to offices and workshops. Locals often head out to the *Kafenia* (coffee houses) to get traditional *Ellinikos kafes* (Greek coffee), Nescafe, refreshing frappes or freddo-cappuccino. The traditional Ellinikos kafes is rich and strong and made in the most curious way. Greek coffee is prepared with or without sugar, never with cream, in a tiny coffee pot called a *briki* on top of a small gas burner. The coffee is brought to a quick boil which forms a creamy froth called *kaimaki* and served in demitasse cups. The sensational sweets in this chapter are especially good with a cup of Greek coffee.

ELLINIKOS KAFES

Greek Coffee

Serves 2

You will need:

§ § § § §

Greek coffee pot
2 cups cold water (Greek coffee cups)
2 teaspoonfuls Greek coffee
Sugar (optional)
2 demitasse coffee cups

§ § § § §

Fill the coffee pot with the cold water. Add the Greek coffee. Add sugar if using and stir just to mix. On high heat bring the coffee to a quick rise, being very careful not to let it boil over. Remove the coffee pot from the heat. Slowly pour some of the froth into each cup. Then pour in the rest of the coffee into each cup and enjoy.

MENTA

Mint Tea

Serves 2

We always had *menta* (fresh mint) growing in the garden when I was young. My mother always rubbed the leaves on us to keep the mosquitoes away. When boiled, it is a great home remedy for upset stomachs. Fresh chopped mint is used in many Greek dishes and makes flavorful *keftedes* (meatballs). It makes a delicious cup of hot tea or a refreshing iced tea.

You will need:

§ § § § § §

1 bunch fresh mint, rinsed

§ § § § § §

In a small boiling pot or tea kettle, bring cold water and a few mint leaves, more or less depending how strong you like it, to a boil. Reduce the heat and simmer for about 5 minutes. Remove from heat and strain. Pour into dainty tea cups and serve along with some delicious paximadia or dipping cookies.

Variation: To make iced mint tea; boil and then cool and strain the tea. Refrigerate until well chilled. Serve in tall iced tea glasses filled with plenty of ice. Garnish with fresh sprigs of mint.

TSOUREKIA TSI ROXANIS

Roxanne's Easter Bread
Makes 3 to 4 loafs

This is the traditional sweet bread, similar to brioche. For Easter, tsoureki is usually shaped into rounds or braided loafs sprinkled with sesame and adorned with a shiny red egg symbolizing the resurrection of Christ. This is also the recipe that is made for Christmas and New Year's Eve.

§ § § § §

7 to 8 cups flour

1/2 cup warm water (approximately 110°F)

1 1/2 envelopes active dry yeast (1 1/2 tablespoonfuls)

1 3/4 cups sugar plus 2 teaspoons

1 cup milk

1/2 pound unsalted butter (2 sticks)

5 eggs, room temperature and lightly beaten

1 teaspoon ground makhlepi (optional, found at Greek specialty shops)

1 teaspoon vanilla extract

1 egg beaten

1 tablespoon water, for the egg wash

1/4 cup sesame seeds

§ § § § §

Place 7 cups of the flour in a large bowl and set aside. Fill a large water glass with the water. Add the yeast, 2 teaspoons of the sugar and stir well. Let stand for about 10 minutes or until it comes to a froth. Heat the milk, butter, and 1 3/4 cups of the remaining sugar in a medium-size sauce pan over low heat until warm but not boiling. Remove the pan from the heat. Let it come to lukewarm. Make a well in the center of the flour mixture. Pour in the eggs, yeast mixture, makhlepi if using, vanilla, and the milk mixture. With your hands, work in the flour, then knead the dough adding more of the remaining flour if needed until the mixture begins to form a soft and slightly sticky dough, about 10 minutes. Place the dough in a clean greased bowl. Cover with a kitchen towel and let it rise in a warm place until doubled in bulk, about 2 1/2 hour. Punch down the dough and leave to rise once again, about 1 more hour. Punch down the dough and divide into 3 to 4 equal portions. Take one portion and divide into 3 pieces. Roll each piece into 3 long ropes and shape into a braid. Repeat with the remaining portions. Place the braids on a greased baking tray. Brush with egg wash and sprinkle with sesame seeds. Let the bread rise in the tray, about 1/2 hour. When you are ready to bake the bread preheat the oven to 350°F. Bake for about 30 minutes, or until golden browned. Turn out the bread to a wire rack. Cover the bread with a clean cloth and let cool.

Paximadia

Note: To make *paximadia* (sweet toast rusks), slice day old tsoureki into 1/2 inch thick slices and bake in a preheated 350°F oven, 10 minutes on each side or until golden.

BISCOTTA AMIGTHALOU

Almond Biscotta

Makes about 2 1/2 dozen

These twice-baked biscotta are easy to make and ready in just 1 hour. Lemon peel gives these a real lemon tangy taste. They go great with coffee. I always have extras on hand when I go visiting. Place a few biscotta on a pretty dish and wrap it up in colorful cellophane tied with ribbon to take with you.

§ § § § §

3 cups flour
2 teaspoons baking powder
3 egg yolks
1 whole egg
1 cup sugar
2 teaspoons vanilla
1/2 cup milk
Zest of 1 whole lemon
1 egg white, beaten
1/2 cup sliced almonds

§ § § § §

Line a baking sheet with parchment. Spray with cooking oil and set aside. Whisk the flour and the baking powder in a medium-size bowl and set aside. Combine the egg yolks and the egg in a large bowl and beat with an electric mixer until frothy. Add the sugar and the vanilla and continue beating until the mixture slightly thickens, about 2 to 3 minutes. Gradually add the flour mixture, a cup at a time, alternating with the milk. Add the lemon zest. The dough should be slightly sticky. Divide the dough into two portions. Drop by large tablespoons onto the prepared baking sheet using a rubber spatula and shape into a long log, about 1 inch high and 15 inches long. Brush with egg white. Sprinkle with almonds and bake at 350°F for about 20 minutes, or until lightly golden. Remove the pan from the oven and set aside a few minutes to cool. Slice the logs into 3/4 inch thick diagonal slices. Raise the oven to 375°F and bake 5 minutes more on each side until golden. Place the biscotta to cool.

Note: Place biscotta in airtight containers or cookie tins and store in a dry place for up to 1 month.

LATHOKOULOURA APO TIN CRETE

Cretan Olive Oil Cookies

Makes 4 dozen

I am blessed to have visited the island of Crete. I sailed aboard the Festos Palace, a huge vessel that carried many people and vehicles to the island. As I approached Crete, I was amazed at how huge the island was. There seemed to be no end in sight. My friend Mr. Vavourakis came to pick me up. As you can guess, we headed straight to the *fourno* (the bakery). My mouth watered as I saw the selection of *lathokouloura* (olive oil cookies), *paximadia* (sweet toast rusks) and wonderful breads. The appetizing aromas coming from the ovens were awesome. You wouldn't believe how delicious the cookies made with olive oil are, especially with the olive oil that comes from Crete. This is a recipe for lathokoulouria, the traditional olive oil cookies that my friend Kiria Christina gave me. She described them as "fantastika." They are great with a cup of Greek coffee or tea.

§ § § § §

4 1/2 to 5 cups flour
1 teaspoon baking powder
1 teaspoon baking soda
1/2 teaspoon cinnamon
1/2 teaspoon clove
2 cups light olive oil
1 cup sugar
1/2 cup cognac
1/2 cup orange juice
Approximately 1 cup sesame seeds

§ § § § §

Line 2 baking sheets with parchment and set aside. In a large bowl stir 4 1/2 cups of the flour, baking powder, baking soda, cinnamon, and clove and set aside. In a large bowl, with an electric mixer, slowly mix the olive oil with the sugar until well combined, about 5 minutes. Add cognac and the orange juice and blend well. Stir 4 cups of the flour mixture, one cup at a time, adding more of the reserved flour if needed so that the dough doesn't stick to your hands. Preheat the oven to 350°F. Generously sprinkle a work surface with sesame seeds, adding more when needed. Take pieces of dough, the size of a walnut and shape while rolling the sesame seeds into the dough, forming twists or crescent shape cookies. Arrange on cookie sheets. Bake for approximately 30 minutes, or until golden. Remove the cookies from the oven. Place the trays on a baking rack to cool. Store in airtight containers or cookie tins in a dry cool place.

Biscotta tsi Ntinas

Dina's Biscotta

Makes 3 dozen

This is one of my sister's treasured recipes. The walnuts make these biscotta wonderfully crunchy. You can substitute almonds instead. Biscotta are the classic coffee partner.

§ § § § §

3 1/2 to 4 cups flour

1 teaspoon baking powder

3/4 pound (3 sticks) unsalted butter, room temperature

1 1/2 cups sugar

6 eggs, beaten

1 teaspoon vanilla extract

1 teaspoon lemon extract

1 cup crushed walnuts

§ § § § §

Whisk 3 1/2 cups of the flour and the baking powder together in a medium-size bowl and set aside. Combine the butter and sugar in a large bowl and beat with an electric mixer until fluffy, about 5 minutes. Add the eggs. Add the vanilla and the lemon extract. Gradually beat in the flour mixture, adding more as needed to make a soft and slightly sticky dough. Stir in the walnuts. Cover and refrigerate for 1 hour, or until ready to use.

To make the biscotta: Preheat the oven to 350°F. Line 2 baking sheets with parchment. Divide the dough into three portions. Shape each portion into a long log, about 1 inch high and 15 inches long. Place the logs onto the prepared baking sheets and bake until lightly golden, about 30 minutes. Remove the pan from the oven and set aside a few minutes to cool. Slice the logs into 3/4 inch thick diagonal slices. Raise the oven temperature to 375°F. Place the biscotta back on the baking pan and bake, 5 minutes more on each side, or until golden.

Note: Store extras in cookie tins and keep in a dry place. They are great to have on hand for the unexpected guest.

KOULOURAKIA TSI YIAYIAS

Yiayia's Butter Cookies

Makes 7 dozen

Kourambiedes, Lathokouloura, Koulourakia, Melomakarona

This is a prized recipe of my Yiayia. Although these traditional butter cookies are made for holidays, they are so delicious that I make them anytime of the year. Traditionally, these cookies are sprinkled with sesame seeds, but if you prefer, sprinkle them with sanding sugar or colored sprinkles.

§ § § § §

6 1/2 to 7 cups flour

4 teaspoons baking powder

1 pound sweet butter (room temperature)

2 1/2 cups sugar

6 egg yolks plus 1 whole egg

2 teaspoons vanilla
1 jigger cognac
1 cup warm milk
1 whole egg beaten with 1/4 cup of water for brushing
Sesame seeds for sprinkling

§ § § § § §

Whisk 6 cups of the flour and the baking powder in a medium size bowl and set aside. Combine the butter and the sugar in a large bowl and beat with an electric mixer until creamy, about 10 minutes. Add the yolks one at a time, mixing well after each addition. Add the whole egg. Add vanilla and the cognac. Gradually beat in the flour mixture alternating with the milk, adding more of the remaining flour if needed to make a soft dough. Cover the dough with plastic wrap and chill in the refrigerator 1/2 hour. When ready to bake, preheat the oven to 350°F. Line 2 baking sheets with parchment. Pinch off pieces of dough the size of a walnut and shape into twists. Place about 1 inch apart on the prepared baking sheets. Brush with beaten egg wash and sprinkle with sesame seeds. Place the pans in the oven and bake for approximately 30 minutes, or until golden and crisp. Cool on a baking rack.

Note: Store up to 1 month in airtight container.

KAIK ME YIAOURTI TSI THIAS SOFIAS

Aunt Sofia's Yogurt Pound Cake

Serves 10 to 12

This recipe is from my Thia Sofia, who is from Kefalonia. This cake resembles a moist and delicious pound cake. If you like, go right ahead and swirl in chocolate cocoa powder or chocolate chips, it taste even better. A dollop of crème fraîche is perfect with this dessert.

§ § § § §

3 cups flour

1 teaspoon baking soda

3/4 pound sweet butter, softened

2 cups sugar

6 eggs, separated

1 cup Greek yogurt

1/4 cup orange juice

1 teaspoon vanilla

6 ounces semi-sweet chocolate chips (optional)

1/4 cup cocoa powder (optional)

§ § § § §

Preheat the oven to 350°F. Grease a bunt pan. Whisk the flour and the baking soda in a large bowl and set aside. Combine the butter and sugar in a large bowl and beat with an electric mixer until fluffy, about 10 minutes. Add the egg yolks, one at a time, mixing well after each addition. Gradually add the dry ingredients, alternating with the yogurt, and blend well. Add the orange juice and vanilla. In a separate, chilled, and very dry stainless steel bowl, beat the egg whites until stiff peaks form. Fold the whites into the mixture using a rubber spatula, a third at a time. Fold in the chocolate chips if using. If using cocoa powder, reserve 2 cups of the batter and set aside. Pour the remaining batter into the prepared pan. Mix the reserved 2 cups of batter with 1/4 cup of cocoa powder. Drop by tablespoons into the batter and swirl into the batter using a knife. Place the pan in the oven and bake for 1 hour, or until a cake tester comes out clean. Transfer the pan to a wire rack to cool. When it is cool enough to handle, invert the cake pan over a large plate to unfold. Dust with confectioners' sugar and place the cake on a pretty pedestal cake dish.

Note: This cake will keep well for several days, covered and stored at room temperature or stored in the refrigerator.

6
Sweet Meals

A Greek meal is usually followed by a dish of lavish fruits: grapes, figs, sliced apples, and pears poked with toothpicks. When I was young I remember on hot summer days, we would have chilled watermelon with chunks of feta cheese for dessert. Sometimes we would have a popular refreshment of the traditional vanilla spoon-sweet; a spoonful of a soft and gooey candy-like confectionary served in a refreshing glass of ice cold water. Greek desserts are typically made for holidays, special occasions, and festivals but when I was growing up, we always had dessert because my family loved sweets. Here, in the U.S., all the Greek churches have wonderful festivals during the year, and the church ladies work hard baking a wonderful array of exquisite desserts from phyllo-filled pastries and fantastic nut-cakes to honey-dipped cookies. In Greece, these religious festivals are celebrated all through the year. These festivals are called "panigyria" and are fun for all the family, celebrated with music and dancing and lots of good foods to eat. Some of the best desserts can be found at Premiere-Patisserie, a bustling café and pastry shop situated around the *platea* (the square) in Argostoli. Part of its appeal is the attentive and handsome waiters dressed in crisp-white shirts with black vests. Outdoor seating is available at the platea for people watching and enjoying afternoon refreshments, while indoors offers an elegant and relaxing experience. There are bakery cases glistening with mouth-watering pastries syrup-soaked cakes and Italian gelato. In the cool winter months, I love sitting around the cozy enclosed seating area in the warmth of the patio heaters. The atmosphere here is always lively and the warm loukoumades drizzled with honey and sprinkled with cinnamon and sesame that are served here, only in the cool winter months, are especially good.

KARPOUZI ME FETA

Watermelon and Feta Cheese Fruit Plate

Serves 6

One vivid memory of growing up in Greece is the hot summer days when we would sit outside and enjoy eating refreshing watermelon and feta cheese. Store the watermelon in the refrigerator to let it chill. Cut it into large bite size pieces right before serving.

§ § § § §

1 small watermelon, cooled in the refrigerator
1 pound feta cheese, cut in large chunks

§ § § § §

Cut the cooled watermelon into large bite size pieces. Place the watermelon in a large pretty serving dish. Serve along with chunks of feta cheese. Use frilly toothpicks as utensils.

LOUKOUMADES ME MELI KAI SOSAMI

Fried Fritters with Honey and Sesame

Serves 6 to 8

Loukoumades are fried fritters drizzled with honey and sprinkled with cinnamon. The best I've ever tasted are served at the Premiere Patisirie in Argostoli Square Kefalonia. Here, they are served warm and sprinkled with sesame. If you don't have the chance to go to Kefalonia, go to one of the Greek church festivals. You can be sure to find the church ladies making them. They are a real treat.

§ § § § § §

4 cups flour

1 envelope active dry yeast (1/4 ounce)

1/2 teaspoon baking powder

Pinch of salt

1 cup warm water

4 cups vegetable oil for frying

Honey for garnish

Sesame for garnish

Ground cinnamon for garnish

§ § § § § §

The Batter: Stir together the flour, yeast, baking powder, and salt in a large bowl. Add 1 cup of warm water and mix with your hands to make soft and sticky dough. Cover the bowl with a piece of plastic wrap (sprayed with vegetable shortening). Let the batter rise for 1 hour, until the mixture has formed tiny bubbles.

Make the Loukoumades: Heat the oil in a 2 quart sauce pot over high heat until hot. Carefully drop the dough by tablespoons into the oil, sliding the dough off with your finger. Fry a few at a time, turning the dough-puffs lightly using tongs, about 2 minutes or until golden brown all over. Carefully remove the loukoumades with a slotted spoon and place on paper towels to drain. Repeat until all the dough is used. Place a few loukoumades on individual dessert plates. Drizzle with honey. Sprinkle with cinnamon and sesame seeds. Serve right away while still warm.

Note: You can substitute crushed walnuts for sesame seeds.

BAKLAVA

Syrup Soaked Pastry with Crushed Walnuts and Spices

Makes 24 pieces

Baklava is an exquisite dessert and one that everyone enjoys. Alternating layers of flaky phyllo pastry and a delicious blend of crushed walnuts and spices cut into diamond square pieces makes an elegant presentation. Pistachios can be substituted for walnuts. A scoop of ice cream goes perfect with this dessert.

§ § § § §

For the Syrup:

4 1/2 cups sugar

3 1/2 cups water

1 cinnamon stick

3 teaspoons lemon juice

1/4 cup honey

For the Baklava:

4 cups crushed walnuts

4 teaspoons ground cinnamon

2 teaspoon ground cloves

2 pounds phyllo pastry, preferably fresh, sold at Greek and ethnic specialty stores, thawed according to the package instructions

1 pound unsalted butter, melted for brushing

Fresh mint sprigs for garnish

§ § § § §

The Syrup: Combine the sugar, water, and cinnamon stick in a medium sauce pan. Stir to dissolve the sugar. Bring to a boil. Simmer and cook for 5 minutes. Add the lemon juice and honey. Cook for 5 minutes more. Set aside to cool.

Preheat the oven 325°F. Line a baking sheet or jelly roll pan 14- x 18- x 1-inch with parchment.

Make the Baklava: Mix the walnuts, cinnamon, and cloves together in a bowl and set aside. Brush and layer 16 sheets of the phyllo with butter, keeping the remaining sheets covered with plastic wrap while you work to prevent it from drying out. Spread 1/3 of the nut filling all over the top of 16 sheets of phyllo. Repeat with 6 more sheets of phyllo, and spread 1/3 of the nut filling over the top. Repeat once again with 6 sheets phyllo and spread the remaining nut mixture. Butter and layer the remaining sheets of phyllo. Brush the baklava with the remaining butter. Cut the baklava into diamond-shape pieces. Place the baklava in the oven and bake for 30 minutes. Turn the oven down to 325°F and bake for 30 minutes more or until golden. Remove the pan from the oven. Slowly drizzle cooled syrup over hot baklava, tilting the pan from side to side until all the syrup is absorbed. Serve in individual paper baking cups or on pretty dessert dishes. Garnish with fresh mint sprigs.

REVANI

Syrup-Soaked Farina Cake
Makes 24 diamond-shape pieces

This is a syrup-soaked cake made with farina. Like many Greek desserts, these are made for special occasions and holidays. Get a head start and make this cake a day in advance so that the syrup soaks into the flavorful cake. To serve, garnish each piece with a half of a maraschino cherry and place in individual paper or foil baking cups.

§ § § § §

1 cup flour

2 cups farina, or Greek semolina (found at Greek specialty shops)

3 teaspoons baking powder

3/4 pound (3 sticks) unsalted butter, softened

1 cup sugar

6 eggs, separated

1 cup warm milk

1 teaspoon vanilla

1 teaspoon brandy

1 tablespoon orange zest

1/2 cup sliced almonds for garnish (optional),

Maraschino cherries, sliced in half, for garnish (optional)

Syrup:

3 cups sugar

11/2 cups water

2 teaspoons fresh lemon juice

1 teaspoon vanilla

§ § § § §

Preheat oven 350°F. Butter a 13- by 9-inch cake pan. Sift the flour, farina, and the baking powder into a large bowl. Set it aside. Combine the butter and the sugar in a large bowl and beat with an electric mixer until creamy. Add the egg yolks, one at a time, mixing well after each addition. Gradually add the dry ingredients alternating with the milk. Add the vanilla and brandy and the orange zest. In a separate chilled and very dry stainless steel bowl, beat the egg whites until stiff peaks form. Fold the whites into the mixture using a rubber spatula, a third at a time. Pour the batter into the prepared pan. Sprinkle with sliced almonds. Place the cake in the oven and bake for 1 hour, or until the cake is lightly golden. Remove the pan from the oven. Place on a wire rack to cool to room temperature.

While the cake is cooling, prepare the syrup. Bring the sugar and water to a boil in a medium saucepan. When syrup comes to a boil, reduce the heat to low. Add the lemon juice and the vanilla. Simmer for 5 minutes. Cut the cake in the pan, into diamond shaped pieces. Slowly pour the hot syrup over the cooled cake. Set the cake aside to soak up the syrup, about 2 hours.

EK-MEK

Kadaifi with Cream

Makes about 12 pieces

In Greece there are a variety of luscious pastries. Ek-Mek is pastry made with a shredded phyllo pastry called kadaifi that is soaked in syrup and layered with a creamy filling and a whipped cream topping which makes this dish absolutely yummy. This dessert is best prepared a day ahead. Store it in the refrigerator to let it set. Garnish each piece with sliced almonds and a maraschino cherry half when ready to serve.

§ § § § §

The Cream Filling:

1 cup flour

1 cup sugar

6 cups cold milk

2 teaspoons vanilla

The Whipped Cream:

2 cups heavy cream

3 tablespoons confectioners' sugar

1 teaspoon vanilla

The Syrup:

2 cups sugar

2 cup water

3 teaspoons lemon juice

The Phyllo Pastry:

1 pound kadaifi phyllo pastry, sold at Greek specialty stores, thawed according to the package instructions

1/4 pound (1 stick) unsalted butter, melted

Slivered almonds for garnish

Maraschino cherries, halved for garnish (optional)

§§§§§§

Make the Cream Filling: Combine the flour, sugar, milk, and vanilla in a medium size saucepan and whisk well. Cook over medium-high heat stirring constantly for 10 minutes or until the cream has thickened like pudding. Remove the pan from the heat. Place the cream in a stainless steel bowl and set aside to cool.

Make the Whipped Cream: Whip the cream in a chilled bowl of an electric mixer on medium-high speed until stiff, but not dry. Fold in the confectioners' sugar and the vanilla. Keep chilled until ready to use.

Make the Syrup: Combine the sugar and water in a medium sauce pan. Stir to dissolve the sugar. Bring to a boil. Simmer and cook for 5 minutes. Add the lemon juice and cook for 5 minutes more. Set aside to cool.

Make the Pastry: Preheat the oven to 325°F. Line a 13- x 9- x 2-inch baking pan with parchment. Pull apart the phyllo pastry and spread it out evenly into the baking pan. With a pastry brush, drizzle the melted butter all over the kataifi pastry. Place the pan in the oven and bake for 15 minutes, or until the pastry is just beginning to color. Remove the pan from the oven. Carefully drizzle the cooled syrup all over the warm pastry and allow it to soak through. When it is completely absorbed, cover with a piece of plastic wrap and store at room temperature for at least 1 hour. Spread with a layer of cream filling evenly over the pastry. Spread with a layer of whipped cream. Cover and place in the refrigerator to set for 24 hours. Cut into squares and serve chilled. Garnish each piece with a few almonds or cherries.

KARITHOPITA

Nut Cake

Makes 24 diamond shape pieces

Nut cakes were made since the Byzantine times. This is one of my Yiayias secret recipes. In this nut lover's recipe, crushed walnuts and aromatic spices incorporate all the ingredients of the ancient past. Traditionally, karithopita is cut into diamond shape pieces. Although this is a syrup soaked cake, it's just as good without the syrup dusted with confections sugar.

§ § § § § §

4 cups walnuts, finely chopped

1 teaspoons ground cinnamon

1 teaspoon ground clove

2 cups flour

4 teaspoons baking powder

1 pound unsalted butter, softened

3 cups sugar

10 eggs, separated

1 teaspoon vanilla

Syrup:

2 cups sugar

4 cups water

1 cinnamon stick

1 teaspoon vanilla

2 teaspoons fresh lemon juice

§ § § § § §

Preheat oven to 350°F. Grease and flour a 13- x 9- x 2-inch cake pan. Mix the walnuts, cinnamon, and clove in a large bowl and set aside. In another bowl, mix the flour with the baking powder and set aside. Combine the butter and the sugar in a large bowl and beat with an electric mixer until light and fluffy, about 10 minutes. Add the egg yolks, one at a time, mixing well after each addition. Gradually add the dry ingredients. Stir in the walnut mixture and vanilla. In a separate chilled and very dry stainless steel bowl, beat the egg whites until stiff peaks form. Fold the whites into the mixture using a rubber spatula, 1/3 at a time. Pour the batter evenly into the prepared baking pan. Place the pan in the oven and bake 1 hour, or until the cake pulls away from the edges and a knife inserted in the center comes out clean. Set aside to cool on a baking rack until it reaches room temperature.

Make the Syrup: Combine the sugar, water, cinnamon stick, and vanilla in a saucepan. Bring to a boil, add the lemon juice and simmer for 10 minutes. Remove from heat. Cut the cake into diamond shape pieces while still in the cake pan. Slowly ladle the hot syrup over the cooled cake, allowing it to seep in before adding more syrup. Cover and set the cake aside for 2 hours before serving. Place each piece in individual paper baking cups.

Note: This cake can be place in an airtight container and stored in the refrigerator for up to 5 days.

KOURAMBIEDES

Wedding Cookies

Makes 45 cookies

Kourambiedes are traditional Greek wedding cookies. These delicate butter cookies are visually stunning treats. These melt-in-your mouth cookies are fragrantly scented with clove. Immediately after baking, heavily dust the cookies with confectioners' sugar and place in pretty colored or foil baking cups. For festive occasions, dust the tops with colored sugar sprinkles. They make an elegant presentation to any buffet table.

§ § § § § §

Confectioners' sugar for dusting

4 cups flour

1/2 teaspoon baking powder

1/2 teaspoon ground clove

1 pound unsalted butter, room temperature

1/2 cup confectioners' sugar

2 egg yolks

2 teaspoons vanilla

1 jigger cognac

1 cup crushed almonds (optional)

§ § § § § §

Line 2 baking sheets with parchment and set aside. Sift confectioners' sugar onto a large sheet of parchment paper or wax paper and set aside. Whisk the flour, baking powder, and clove in a medium size bowl and set aside. Whip the butter in a large bowl with an electric mixer until creamy, about 10 minutes. Slowly add the sugar and beat until fluffy. Add the egg yolks, one at a time and mix well. Add the vanilla and cognac. Gradually beat in 3 cups of the flour mixture, a cup at a time, on low speed until the dough is soft and slightly sticky. Remove the bowl from the mixer. By hand, mix in enough of the remaining flour so that the dough doesn't stick to your hands. Stir in the almonds if using. Preheat the oven to 325°F. Pinch off walnut size pieces of dough and shape into small S shape crescents or shape into slightly flattened rounds. Place the cookies on the prepared baking pans 1/2 inch apart and bake for approximately 30 minutes, or until lightly colored, not brown. Remove the cookies from oven. Carefully place the warm cookies on the prepared paper, which has been sifted with confectioners' sugar. Sift the tops with a heavy coating of confectioners' sugar. Place the cookies in individual paper baking cups.

Note: These cookies can be stored in an airtight container in a cool dry place for 3 weeks.

MELOMAKARONA

Honey Dipped Cookies

Makes 4 dozen

This is an old-fashioned cookie recipe. For this spice lover's cookie, olive oil, cinnamon and clove make these ancient spice cookies unbelievably delicious. Grated orange peel adds a little zest. They are made moist by dipping them in fragrant syrup and garnished with a walnut-cinnamon mixture.

§ § § § §

4 cups flour
1 teaspoon baking powder
1/2 cup farina
1 teaspoon cinnamon
1 teaspoon clove
2 cups light olive oil
1 cup sugar
1 teaspoon baking soda
1 cup orange juice
1 jigger cognac
1 teaspoon vanilla
1 tablespoon orange zest

Mixture of 1 cup chopped walnuts combines with 2 teaspoons cinnamon and clove for garnish

Syrup:

2 cups water
2 cups sugar
1 cup honey
1 cinnamon stick
3 whole cloves
Juice of 1/2 lemon

§ § § § §

Line 2 cookie sheets with parchment and set aside. Whisk the flour, baking powder, farina, cinnamon, and clove together in a large bowl and set aside. Combine the olive oil and the sugar in a mixing bowl. At low speed, blend well with an electric mixer. Dissolve the baking soda in the orange juice and mix into batter. Add the cognac, vanilla, and zest. Stir in the flour mixture, one cup at a time, to form soft dough. Preheat the oven to 350F. Shape 1 tablespoonful of the dough at a time into small oval or egg shaped cookies, about 2 inches long, and place on the prepared cookie pans. Bake 20 minutes, or until lightly golden. Remove the cookie sheets from the oven and place on a baking rack to cool. Combine water, sugar, honey, cinnamon stick, and cloves in a medium saucepan and bring to a boil. Add the lemon juice. Reduce the heat and simmer, 5 minutes. With a slotted spoon, dip the cooled cookies, one at a time into the warm syrup. Place the cookies in individual paper or foil baking cups. Sprinkle the cookies with the walnut mixture.

RIZATHA

Rice Pudding

Serves 4

At my restaurant customers request rice pudding when they make their reservation. This surprisingly creamy pudding is a popular dessert and one that everyone enjoys. It is usually served chilled and sprinkled with cinnamon. However, it's especially good served warm. Golden raisins complement this pudding.

§ § § § § §

4 cups whole milk
1/2 cup sugar
1 tablespoon butter
1 cinnamon stick
1/2 cup rice
1 egg
1 cup light cream
1 teaspoon vanilla
1/2 cup golden raisins (optional)
Ground cinnamon, for garnish

§ § § § § §

Combine the milk, sugar, butter, and cinnamon stick in a medium sauce pot. Bring to a boil over medium-high heat. Add the rice. Simmer, stirring frequently with a wooden spoon until the rice is tender, about 45 minutes. In a medium size bowl, whisk the egg. Whisk in the cream. Remove the pot from the heat. Slowly pour the egg mixture into the pot. Return the pot to the heat. Add the vanilla and the raisins if using and stir. Continue cooking over low heat until the pudding has thickened, about 5 minutes more. Remove from the heat. Discard the cinnamon stick. Pour into individual dessert cups and sprinkle with cinnamon.

7
The Sea, The Sea

Argostoli's Natural Harbor

Argostoli is Kefalonias' charming port and bustling town set along the natural harbor. It's a sort of place that I never tire of. It has all the European charm. Across from the harbor is the local bus station (KTEL), banks, bakeries and boutique hotels. There are stylish patisseries that sell meltingly delicious desserts and unique island treats like mandoles (red candy-coated almonds) and mandolato (almond nugget). Curb side kiosk sell everything but the kitchen sink, from cigarettes to newspapers. To the rear is the cosmopolitan Lithostroto, an outdoor shopping area with souvenir shops and cafe bars where crowds gather or promenade along. Beside the harbor is the Koutavos lagoon, a lovely park setting where birds migrate and swans go swimming. There are seaside tavernas, outdoor farmers' markets that sell the islands fruits and vegetables and kafenios (coffee houses). Caretta-Caretta (Loggerhead) sea turtles, colossal yachts and glass bottom boats are some of the beauties that adorn the palm tree-lined harbor. In the early mornings, this is where the locals gather to buy the finest selection of fish from the fishermen. The skyline view is the most beautiful view in the world. Just across from the harbor is Mr. Grillo's Taverna. It's an open-air place with wooden chairs and tables lined with paper tablecloths and an attentive wait staff. This is my favorite place to eat on the island that serves super-fresh fish that is bought from the dock. Here, you can walk up to the grand, open kitchen to see the display of all the delicious home style dishes. This is where tourists and locals come to eat good Greek food. Everything tastes so good here. The sweet and flavorful *barbounia* (red mullet) and *pan-fried marides* (picarel) are the best I have ever tasted. This is a perfect place with a breathtaking view to enjoy a savory seafood meal.

MARITHES TIGANITES

Pan Fried Picarel
Serves 4

Marides are like tiny fish, similar to smelts. They are popular on menus especially at most seaside tavernas throughout Greece. These tiny fish are prepared pan-fried and crispy. Serve with fresh boiled greens and fried potatoes.

§ § § § § §

1 pound smelts, washed, cleaned, and heads removed

Pinch of salt and pepper

Approximately 1 cup flour for dredging

1 cup olive oil for frying

Fresh parsley sprigs for garnish

1 lemon cut into wedges

§ § § § § §

Season the smelts with salt and pepper. Lightly dredge the smelts in flour and shake off excess. Heat the oil in a large frying pan over medium-high heat until hot, but not smoking. Carefully place the smelts, a few at a time, in the pan. Fry for 1 to 2 minutes on each side, until golden and crisp. Carefully remove smelts and drain on paper towels. Place the smelts on a serving dish. Garnish with parsley sprigs and lemon wedges. A chilled glass of Robolla wine will complement this dish.

BAKALIAROS TIGANITO

Fried Cod Fish

Serves 4

This is a favorite dish in Greece. Bakaliaros is salted cod fish that is pan fried until golden and crisp. Although this dish is usually accompanied by the garlicky skordalia potatoes, fried potatoes work well, too.

§§§§§§

1 cup flour
2 tablespoons corn starch
1 1/2 pounds dried salted cod fish, pre-soaked (see note)
1 cup vegetable oil
1 lemon cut in wedges
1 recipe Skordalia (page 50)

§§§§§§

In a large bowl whisk together the flour and the cornstarch and set aside. Drain the cod and cut into 4 serving pieces. Lightly dredge the cod in the flour mixture and shake off excess. Heat the oil in a large skillet or frying pan over medium-high heat until hot, but not smoking. Carefully place the cod in the pan and fry, turning once, until golden and crisp on both sides, about 5 minutes per side. Drain on absorbent paper. Garnish with lemon wedges and serve warm along with skordalia and a chilled glass of Robolla wine.

Note: It is necessary to soak the salted cod fish in cold water for about 24 hours, changing the water every 3 hours to remove the salt from the fish.

KALAMARI TIGANITO

Fried Calamari

Serves 4

These tender rings of fried squid are a favorite mezé, or appetizer, on most menus in Greek tavernas. I like to serve them accompanied by tzatziki sauce for dipping.

§ § § § §

3/4 cup flour
1/4 cup corn starch
Vegetable oil for frying
1 to 1 1/2 pounds fresh squid, cleaned, rinsed and cut into tiny rings
1 fresh lemon cut in half
Salt and pepper to taste
2 teaspoons dried Greek oregano
Lemon wedges for garnish
Sprigs of fresh flat-leaf or curly parsley
Tzatziki Sauce (optional) (see page 139)

§ § § § §

Combine the flour and cornstarch in a medium bowl and mix well. Heat enough vegetable oil to come to 1 inch in a large frying pan or skillet over medium-high heat until hot, but not smoking. In batches, lightly dredge the squid in the flour mixture and shake off excess. Add as many pieces of squid as will fit in the pan without crowding, and fry until crispy and golden all over, about 4 to 5 minutes. Remove the squid with a slotted spoon and drain on paper towels. Repeat with the remaining squid adding more oil if necessary. Place the fried squid in a large bowl. Squeeze the lemon all over. Sprinkle with salt, pepper, and oregano and toss. Place the calamari on a serving dish. Garnish with lemon wedges and parsley. Serve while hot.

GIGANTES PLAKI

Baked Giant Beans

Serves 6 to 8

Gigantes, are "giant beans" that are farmed in the rich fertile soils of northern Greece. They look similar to a large, dry lima bean. In this recipe, gigantes beans are cooked until tender then baked in a rich tomato sauce which makes these beans taste absolutely delicious. Gigantes are best served room temperature as an appetizer or alongside your favorite fish dish. This also makes a great vegetarian dish.

§ § § § § §

1 16-ounce bag dried gigantes beans, soaked overnight in cold water

3 quarts water

1 cup coarsely chopped celery

3 cups coarsely chopped onions

1 bay leaf

1/3 cup chopped parsley

1/2 cup tomato paste

1/2 teaspoon dried Greek oregano

3 garlic cloves, whole

1/2 cup olive oil, plus more for drizzling

Salt to taste

1/4 teaspoon white pepper

2 carrots, peeled and coarsely chopped

§ § § § § §

Place the beans in a large pot. Add the water and bring to a boil. Add the celery, onions, bay leaf, parsley, tomato paste, and oregano. Reduce heat to medium and cook until just tender, about 1 hour. Preheat the oven to 375°F. Stir in the garlic, olive oil, salt, pepper, and carrots. Taste for seasoning. Remove the pot from the heat. Carefully place the beans in a medium baking pan. Cover with foil and bake for 1 hour, or until the beans are tender and the sauce has thickened. Remove the pan from the oven. Set the pan aside to cool to room temperature. Place the beans on individual appetizer dishes. Drizzle with olive oil and serve accompanied by plenty of fresh bread and feta cheese.

Note: If you like to cook the beans the same day and don't have time to soak them overnight, place the beans in a large pot with enough water to cover and bring to a boil. Set the beans aside for 1 to 2 hours. Then, drain the beans and cook according to the directions above.

PSARI TIS SKARAS

Grilled Whole Fish

Serves 4

Grilling fish is an ancient Greek tradition. At my restaurant, I serve fresh, whole fish flown in from Greece. *Dorade* (tsiporas) is a mild, white fish, one of the most highly prized fish from the Mediterranean Sea. Simply marinated with lots of fresh lemon and olive oil and grilled to perfection. This fish is similar to sea bass. Red mullet is also a good choice.

§ § § § § §

4 whole fish (about 1 pound each)
1 recipe Latho-Lemono Dressing (see page 121)
1 teaspoon dried Greek oregano
1 lemon, cut into wedges

§ § § § § §

Rinse the fish under cold water. Place the fish in a large baking sheet and pat dry. Score the fish making several diagonal slashes approximately 1/4 inch deep. Heat the grill or broiler. Brush the fish with 1/2 of the dressing and place on the grill or directly on the grate or broiler platter under the broiler. Grill or broil the fish for 8 to 10 minutes, until lightly charred on one side. Turn and grill or broil for 8 to 10 minutes more, or until cooked through. Place the fish on individual dishes and spoon the remaining marinade over the fish. Sprinkle with oregano. Serve garnished with the lemon wedges and accompanied by roasted Greek potatoes.

KAKAVIA

Fish Soup

Serves 2

Similar to the French bouillabaisse, this soup is filled with flavors of the sea. Although this is a classic all over Greece, it is a real favorite on all the Greek Islands where fresh fish is plentiful. For this soup, you could be as lavish as you like. Instead of shrimp, you can use langoustines, which are small North Atlantic lobsters.

§ § § § §

4 cups fish or vegetable stock

2 tablespoons olive oil

1/2 small onion, halved lengthwise and thinly sliced

1 small leek, rinsed well of all the sandy soil, white and light green parts, cut into thin julienne sticks

1 small carrot, peeled and cut into thin julienne sticks

6 garlic cloves, minced

2 sundried tomatoes, thinly sliced

1/2 pound fresh sea scallops, preferably dry

1/2 pound fresh large shrimp, peeled and deveined

1/2 pound fresh white fish, such as flounder or cod, cut into bite size pieces

1/2 pound clams (little neck), well scrubbed

1/2 pound mussels, de-bearded and scrubbed

Juice of 1/2 lemon

Salt, white pepper to taste

4 crustini toasts for garnish

§ § § § §

Pour the stock in a large soup pot or casserole and bring to a boil. Add the olive oil, onions, leeks, carrots, garlic, and tomatoes. Reduce the heat to medium and cook until the vegetables are soft, about 15 minutes. Add the scallops, shrimp, and white fish to the pot. Cover the pot and continue cooking, about 5 minutes. Add the clams and mussels and cook until the shells open and fish filets are firm, about 5 minutes more. Add the lemon juice, salt, and pepper. Taste for seasoning. Serve the fish in 4 large soup bowls. Ladle the soup and serve the vegetables on top. Garnish each with crustini toast and serve hot.

TARAMOSALATA

Greek Caviar Dip

Serves 6 to 8

A Greek classic, this creamy caviar dip is made with orange colored carp roe, potatoes, onions, lemon juice and olive oil. In Greece this appetizer is always garnished with an olive. Serve accompanied by fresh bread or warm pita wedges.

§ § § § § §

2 medium Idaho potatoes, peeled and cut into 1/2 inch pieces
1/2 cup finely chopped onions
1/2 cup lemon juice
1 cup olive oil
1/4 cup *tarama* (carp roe), found in Greek specialty shops
Extra virgin olive oil for drizzling
Kalamata olives for garnish

§ § § § § §

Place the potatoes in a medium pot. Cover with water, and bring to a boil. Simmer and cook until the potatoes are tender, but not overcooked, about 10 minutes. Drain the potatoes well in a colander and cool to room temperature. Place them in the refrigerator to cool completely, about 1 hour. Once cooled, place the potatoes, onions, and lemon juice into a food processor. Pulverize the mixture using the pulse on and off method until well blended. Gradually drizzle in the olive oil. Add the tarama and pulse into a smooth mixture. Place the mixture into the refrigerator to chill. When ready to serve, place on a pretty serving dish. Drizzle with extra-virgin olive oil. Garnish with kalamata olives.

XTAPODI SALATA

Octopus Salad with Fresh Field Greens and Lentils

Serves 4

Offer this octopus as a perfect light meal atop a bed of fresh field greens with lentils in lemon vinaigrette or right off the grill like they do in Greece as a mezé with a wedge of lemon. A glass of Plomariou Ouzo on the rocks goes along well with this.

§ § § § §

Approximately 2 pounds, fresh octopus, or frozen (completely defrosted)

Approximately 2 to 3 cups of water

1 cup vinegar

1 bay leaf

Latho-Lemono Dressing

1/4 cup olive oil

Juice of one whole lemon

1/2 teaspoon salt

1 teaspoon dried Greek oregano

The Salad:

1 (10-ounce) bag of fresh field greens
1/2 cup cooked brown lentils, preferably Greek or French
Lemon wedges for garnish

§ § § § § §

Rinse the octopus and place it in a large pot. Add the water, just enough to cover, vinegar and the bay leaf. Cook partially covered over medium-high heat until tender when the tentacle pulls off easily with tongs. Remove the octopus from the heat. Drain in a colander and cool. If using small octopus, you can cut them in half or leave them whole. If using large octopus, separate the tentacles. Heat a grill or broiler. Place the octopus on the grill or directly on the grate or broiler plate under the broiler. Grill or broil the octopus for 2 to 3 minutes on each side to produce grill marks.

Make the Latho-Lemono Dressing: In a medium size bowl, whisk the olive oil, lemon juice, salt and oregano and set aside.

Make the salad: Place the field greens and the lentils in a large bowl. Add the octopus and the dressing and toss. Place the salad on individual appetizer dishes. Garnish with lemon wedges.

FILETO SOLOMOS PANE ME DOMATA, CAPARI KAI ILIES

Pan Seared Salmon with Chopped Tomatoes, Capers and Kalamata Olives

Serves 4

I prefer the wonderful flavor of the wild Alaskan salmon that comes from the clean waters of Alaska. Salmon is a super-food with high protein and omega 3 fatty acids. Chopped tomatoes, Kalamata olives and capers give this dish a superb flavor. Mashed potatoes or rice pilaf go great with this dish. You could also use filet of halibut or flounder.

§ § § § §

4 salmon filets, about 4 ounces each

1/2 teaspoon salt

1/4 teaspoon pepper

2 tablespoons olive oil

1/2 cup dry white wine

1/2 cup fish stock (see page 125)

Juice of 1/2 lemon

2 tablespoons butter

1 cup chopped tomatoes

1/4 cup Kalamata olives or other brine-cured black olives

1/4 cup capers

§ § § § §

Rinse the salmon and pat dry. Season the fish with salt and pepper. Heat the oil in a large skillet over medium-high heat until hot, but not smoking. Add salmon fillets and sear on both sides until lightly browned and just cooked through, about 5 minutes. Add the wine and increase the heat to high. Cook for 1 minute. Add stock, lemon, butter, and tomatoes and bring the liquid to a boil. Reduce the heat to low and simmer for 3 minutes or until the sauce thickens. Add olives and capers. Taste and correct the seasonings. Place the fish fillets onto 4 serving plates. Spoon the sauce over the fish and serve warm accompanied by rice pilaf or mashed potatoes.

XTENIA SAUTÉ ME ASPRO KRASI

Sautéed Sea Scallops in a White Wine Sauce

Serves 4 (appetizer portions)

The most delicious sea scallops are the ones that are shucked on board the scallop boats and packed right away without any preservatives. These are called "dry scallops." These scallops have a tender and sweet flavor. Serve these alone as an appetizer or as an entrée accompanied by rice and steamed broccoli or sautéed baby spinach.

§ § § § § §

2 tablespoons olive oil
1 pounds dry sea scallops
1 garlic clove finely chopped
1/2 cup dry white wine
1/4 cup fish stock (see page 125)
2 teaspoons fresh lemon juice
Salt and pepper to taste
1 tablespoon butter

§ § § § § §

Heat the oil in a large sauté pan over high heat until hot, but not smoking. Reduce the heat to medium. Using tongs, add the scallops and sear without turning, until well browned on one side, about 3 minutes. Add the garlic and wine, and cook until the liquid is reduced, 1 to 2 minutes. Add stock, lemon, salt, pepper, and butter and sauté, shaking the pan until the liquid has thickened and is sauce like, 2 minutes more. Taste and adjust the seasonings. Arrange a few scallops on individual appetizer dishes. Drizzle the sauce over the scallops. Serve immediately while hot.

ZOMOS PSARI

Fish Stock

Makes about 1 1/2 quart

You can use fish stock to make a more flavorful fish dish, or to make fish soup like Kakavia. It's simple and easy to make in less than one hour. Just ask your fish monger for fresh bones from lean fish such as flounder, whiting or sole.

§ § § § §

2 pounds fresh lean fish bones such as, flounder, sole or whiting, rinsed thoroughly in cold water

2 quarts cold water

1 stalk celery, diced in small pieces

1 carrot, peeled and diced

1 large onion, peeled and diced

Sachet: 1 bay leaf, 3 whole peppercorns, 1/2 teaspoon dried thyme, 2 to 3 fresh flat leaf or curly parsley stems

§ § § § §

Combine all the ingredients in a stock pot. Bring to a simmer and skim off foam from the surface of the stock. Cook, uncovered for about 45 minutes. Allow to cool thoroughly. Strain the stock. You can refrigerate leftovers for up to 2 days.

MELINTZANES TIGHANITES

Pan Fried Eggplant

Serves 4 to 6

Here's an appetizing starter. These thinly sliced eggplant slices are tenderly fried and pair great with fried zucchini slices. They are best served warm as soon as they are made. Serve accompanied by tzatziki sauce.

§ § § § § §

2 cups flour
1/2 cup corn starch
Pinch of salt and pepper
1 large eggplant, about 1 pound, stem ends cut off and sliced into 1/4 inch thick rounds
1 teaspoon salt for soaking
1 to 1 1/2 cups vegetable oil for frying

§ § § § § §

Line a baking sheet with parchment and set aside. Combine the flour, cornstarch, salt and pepper in a large bowl and mix well. Place the eggplant slices in a large bowl. Add the salt and enough cold water to cover. Set a plate over the bowl to keep the eggplants submerged. Set aside for 1/2 hour. Drain the eggplants. Dredge each eggplant slice in the flour mixture and shake off excess. Arrange in a single layer on the baking sheet. Add oil to 1/4 inch in a large frying pan. Heat over medium-high heat until hot, but not smoking. Fry the eggplant slices, a few at a time, until golden, about 2 minutes each side. Place on paper towels to drain. Arrange the eggplant slices on a serving platter. Serve immediately.

Kolokithakia Tiganita

Note: To make *kolokithakia tiganita* (fried zucchini), use 3 to 4 medium zucchini (about 1 pound) washed, trimmed and cut lengthwise into 1/4-inch thick slices. Dredge each zucchini slice in the flour mixture and follow the directions above.

8
The Restaurant

Lourdas Greek Taverna. It flows with the traditional Greek excitement. I should have put a movie camera in the kitchen; it definitely would have been movie material. In February of 1999, I decided that I wanted to open a restaurant. I loved to cook; it was my passion, my hobby, and it was what I did best. I did all my homework. The most interesting thing is that I've educated myself in cooking. Yiayia was the main ingredient. From the many trips to Greece, I've absorbed as much as I could. I read and made almost all the recipes in my Bon Appetite magazines. Either you have it or you don't. And now this is the consequence. I didn't have much money. My daughter and I wrote a business plan and after many months I was granted the business loan. I launched a search for the perfect location in Bryn Mawr, Pennsylvania. I had a budget to work with, so, I bought used equipment from a repo man, and went to New York's China town district to buy dining room furniture. By the time we transformed our space into a restaurant, we were exhausted! It was December 26, 2000 when we had our grand opening. We hadn't slept in days. Lourdas is like the mom and pop restaurant with no pop. It's a Greek family restaurant with a blue and white scene; the kind of taverna you'd find in the Greek islands. We have become Bryn Mawr's best kept secret. We make Greek food the old fashioned way, everything is homemade. Together, my children and I have introduced authentic Greek food to a wide and appreciative group of diners. We all worked so hard and many long hours. Now, I am writing this book so that you can enjoy some of the best recipes from our restaurant.

ZOMOS KOTAS

Chicken Stock

Makes about 1 quart

For a more flavorful dish, use chicken stock instead of water when you're making favorite chicken dishes. I like to keep chicken stock in the freezer and take it out when I need it. What's really great is to make chicken stock ice cubes and then store them in baggies in the freezer. Take out as many as you need to add flavor to your favorite sauce or rice dish.

§ § § § §

2 pounds raw chicken back bones, rinsed in cold water

2 quarts cold water

1 large onion, halved and thickly sliced

1 carrot, peeled and chopped

1 rib celery, chopped

Sachet: 1 bay leaf, pinch dried thyme, 2 black peppercorns, 2 to 3 parsley stems, tied in a pouch of cheesecloth with butchers twine

§ § § § §

Place the chicken bones in a stock pot and cover them with cold water. Bring to a boil. Reduce the heat to a simmer skimming off the foam from the surface of the stock. Add the onions, carrot, and celery and the sachet to the stock. Reduce the heat to simmer for about 3 hours. Strain the stock. Allow to cool thoroughly. You can refrigerate leftovers for up to 2 days.

SAGANAKI OPA!

Fried Cheese Flambé

Serves 2 to 3

Saganaki takes its name from the two-handled pan in which it is cooked. In most Greek restaurants in the United States, sharp kefalotiri cheese, similar to Parmesan, is sautéed in a small oval skillet until soft, drizzled with ouzo or cognac, and served flambé. As the cheese is brought out to the table the servers excitedly shout, "OPA!" Saganaki is just as good without the flambé.

§ § § § §

1/2 pound kefalotiri cheese or kefalograviera, found in Greek specialty shops
Flour for dredging
2 tablespoons olive oil
Jigger of ouzo or cognac
Fresh flat-leaf or curly parsley sprigs for garnish
1 small lemon, cut into wedges

§ § § § §

Cut the cheese into 2 to 3 1/2 inch slice rectangles. Rinse the cheese in cold water to remove excess salt, and pat dry with paper towels. Dredge lightly with flour. Heat the olive oil in a medium-size nonstick skillet or frying pan until hot, but not smoking. Place the cheese slices in the skillet. Sauté on medium-high heat until the cheese softens, turning once until lightly golden but not browned on both sides, about 2 minutes per side. Arrange the cheese on a heat proof dish. Drizzle with ouzo or cognac, if desired, and serve flambé garnished with parsley sprigs and lemon wedges.

GARIDES LOURDAS

Sautéed Shrimp with Chopped Tomatoes and Feta

Serves 4

    This is one of Lourdas' signature shrimp dishes. I always buy fresh Mexican shrimp which have a slightly sweet flavor. Just before serving add the feta cheese until it softens. This dish pairs perfectly with rice.

§ § § § §

3 tablespoons olive oil

1 1/2 pounds large shrimp, peeled and deveined, tails left on

1 cup dry white wine

2 cups fish stock (see page 125)

1 cup chopped tomatoes

1/2 cup chopped scallions, white and green parts

3 tablespoons fresh lemon juice

Salt and pepper to taste

1 cup feta cheese, crumbled

§ § § § § §

Heat the oil in a large frying pan over medium-high heat until hot, but not smoking. Add the shrimp to the pan and cook, tossing the shrimp just until the shrimp are pink, about 5 minutes. Add the wine and steam off. Add the stock, tomatoes, scallions, and lemon. Season the shrimp with salt and pepper. Simmer for 2 to 3 minutes or until the sauce begins to thicken. Stir in the feta cheese, and simmer 1 minute more, or until the feta softens. Remove the pan from the heat. Divide the shrimp among dinner plates. Spoon the sauce over the shrimp and serve right away accompanied by rice pilaf.

GREEK SALAD DRESSING

Makes 1 cup

There are no thick and creamy Greek salad dressings. The basic ingredients to the standard Greek salad dressing are the fruity olive oil and vinegar.

§ § § § §

3/4 cup extra-virgin olive oil
1/4 cup vinegar
1 tablespoon fresh lemon juice
3 to 4 cloves garlic, minced
1 teaspoon dried Greek oregano
Salt and pepper to taste

§ § § § §

In a small bowl, whisk together all of the above ingredients. Transfer the dressing to a salad bottle. Use right away, or store in the refrigerator for up to 3 days.

PATATES TIGANITES

Fried Potatoes

Serves 2 to 4

At Greek tavernas in Greece, the main meal consists of assorted appetizers, hot and cold. They are brought out to the table one by one as soon as they are prepared. *Patates tiganites* are among these mezethes. These potatoes are delicious seasoned with oregano and lemon.

§ § § § § §

Vegetable oil for frying
2 large Idaho potatoes, scrubbed and cut into French fries 3/8- by 3/8- x 3-inch sticks
1/2 of one lemon
Salt and pepper to taste
1 teaspoon dried Greek oregano

§ § § § § §

Pour about 1 inch of the oil in a large frying pan or skillet over medium-high heat until hot, but not smoking. Add the potatoes and fry, until golden brown all over, about 5 minutes. Transfer the potatoes to paper towel to drain. Place the potatoes in a large bowl. Squeeze the lemon all over the potatoes. Sprinkle with salt, pepper, and oregano and toss. Serve right away while hot.

Note: These potatoes can be peeled or prepared with the skins also.

ZOMOS APO LAHANIKA

Vegetable Stock

Makes 4 cups

Vegetable stock is very simple and easy to make. It enhances the flavors when substituting for water in most any dish. You could use it as a base for a vegetarian soup. Just add some small shape pasta, rice or Asian noodles to have a terrific vegetarian bowl of soup.

§ § § § §

1 tablespoon vegetable oil

1 cup diced onions

1/2 cup diced celery

1/2 cup diced carrots

1 garlic clove

2 tablespoons white wine

4 cups cold water

Sachet: 1 bay leave, pinch of dried thyme, 2 black peppercorns, 2 to 3 parsley stems tied together in a piece of cheesecloth

§ § § § §

Heat the oil in a medium-sized stock pot over medium high heat. Add the onions, celery, carrots, and garlic and sauté until soft, about 10 minutes. Add the white wine, water, and sachet. Bring to a boil. Reduce to a simmer and cook for 45 minutes. Strain the stock. Use immediately or cool to room temperature and store in the refrigerator, for up to 3 days.

KRITHERAKI SALATA

Orzo Pasta Salad

Serves 4

Serve this salad for your next barbeque party. Orzo, the tiny, rice-shaped pasta tossed along with sweet grape tomatoes and cucumbers make a colorful presentation. This is a great vegetarian salad. If you prefer, grill some chicken strips. Dice them up and toss them right in.

§ § § § § §

1 cup orzo pasta, cooked according to the package directions and drained

1 medium cucumber, preferably seedless, peeled and diced

1 pint grape tomatoes, sliced in half

1 small red onion, diced

1/4 cup Kalamata olives, pitted and thinly sliced

1/2 cup crumbled feta cheese

1 teaspoon finely chopped cilantro

4 tablespoons Greek Salad Dressing (see page 133)

§ § § § § §

Place the pasta, cucumbers, tomatoes, onions, olives, feta, and cilantro in a large pasta bowl. Pour the salad dressing and toss gently to mix. Cover and chill in the refrigerator until ready to serve.

SOUVLAKI ARNISIO ME RIZI

Skewered Lamb with Rice Pilaf

Serves 4 to 6

Although in Greece simple versions of this dish include only meat on a stick poked with a piece of bread, serve this succulent lamb dish as an entrée with grilled vegetables atop a bed of rice pilaf. This dish is similar to shish kebab. Tzatziki sauce makes a delicious accompaniment.

§ § § § §

Rice Pilaf (see page 141)
1 1/2 to 2 pounds boneless leg of lamb, cut into 2 inch cubes
1 recipe Latho-Lemono Dressing (see page 121)
1 large onion, quartered
2 large bell peppers (about 1 pound), red and green, stemmed, seeded, and cut into 2-inch squares
4 to 6 cherry tomatoes
1 teaspoon Greek oregano
Sprigs of fresh flat-leaf parsley
1 lemon cut into wedges
Tzatziki Sauce (see page 139) optional
4 to 6 skewers

§ § § § §

Make the rice pilaf. Place the lamb pieces on a baking sheet. Add the Latho-Lemono Dressing and turn to coat the lamb with your hands. Heat the grill or broiler. Skewer the lamb pieces alternating with onions and peppers. Pierce each with a cherry tomato. Place the skewers on the grill or directly on the grate or broiler plate under the broiler. Grill or broil the skewers of lamb for 4 to 5 minutes, until lightly charred on one side. Turn and grill or broil for 4 to 5 minutes more (medium rare: 130˚ to 140˚F), or until the desired doneness. Remove the skewers from the grill or broiler. Mound a portion of rice on each individual serving dish. Arrange a skewer on top of the rice. Sprinkle with oregano. Garnish with parsley and lemon wedges and serve while hot.

Souvlaki Kotopoulo me Rizi

Variation: For souvlaki kotopoulo me rizi (chicken), substitute 4 skinless and boneless chicken breast halves, about 2 pounds, rinsed, patted dry and cut into 2 inch pieces. Grill or broil the chicken depending upon the thickness until the meat is firm when touched and springs back quickly when pressed with a finger.

HUMMUS

Chick Pea and Tahini Dip

Serves 4 to 6

Although you can buy hummus at most grocery stores and specialty shops, there's nothing better than homemade. It's quick and simple to make. My best friend Linda Saah first taught me how to make hummus. A surprisingly creamy puree of chickpeas, garlic, tahini, lemon juice and olive oil makes this a delectable dip. At my restaurant I serve hummus as an appetizer with sliced cold cucumbers all around the dish or along with assorted appetizers on the pekelia dish with plenty of warm pita bread for dipping.

§ § § § § §

2 cups canned chick peas, drained
3 tablespoons fresh lemon juice
3 to 4 garlic cloves, minced
2 to 3 tablespoons tahini, found in Greek and ethnic specialty shops and super markets
1/2 teaspoon salt
1/2 cup olive oil

Extra-virgin olive oil for garnish
Chopped fresh flat-leaf or curly parsley for garnish
Cucumber sliced in rounds

§ § § § § §

Place the chickpeas in the food processor. Add the lemon juice, garlic, tahini, salt, and olive oil. Process, 5 minutes, or until the mixture is a smooth and creamy consistency. Taste and adjust the seasonings. Place the hummus on a pretty appetizer dish. Serve chilled, drizzled with olive oil. Garnish with parsley accompanied by cucumber slices and warm pita wedges.

Note: Store leftovers in the refrigerator for up to 2 days.

TZATZIKI

Yogurt Cucumber Dip
Serves 4

Kalamata olives, Taramosalata, Melintzanosalata, Tzatziki, Dolmades and Feta cheese

This is the special Greek sauce made with lots of garlic, Greek yogurt, grated cucumbers, fresh lemon juice, and olive oil. This is best served as an appetizer or accompanied with an assortment of appetizers with plenty of fresh bread or warm pita wedges for dipping or served atop souvlaki or gyros. Substituting sour cream for yogurt is equally good.

§ § § § §

2 cups Greek yogurt

1 medium cucumber (preferably seedless) peeled, coarsely grated and drained

1/4 cup extra-virgin olive oil

1 tablespoon chopped fresh dill (optional)

Pinch of salt

1/4 cup fresh lemon juice

8 cloves garlic, crushed

§ § § § § §

Place the yogurt in a medium bowl. Add the cucumber pulp, olive oil, dill, salt, lemon juice and garlic. Mix until thoroughly combined. Cover and refrigerate. Serve chilled as an appetizer accompanied by plenty of warm pita, or as a condiment along with your favorite meal.

PILAFI

Rice Pilaf

Serves 4

Chicken stock adds wonderful flavor to this rice pilaf. It's quick and easy to make. For a showy presentation, add frozen peas and carrots along with the chicken stock.

§ § § § §

1 tablespoon butter
1/4 cup finely chopped onions
1 cup rice
2 cups hot chicken stock
1 bay leaf
Pinch of salt

§ § § § §

Preheat the oven to 350°F. Melt the butter in a medium sauce pot over medium-high heat. Add the onions and sauté until soft but not brown. Add the rice and stir to coat. Add the chicken stock. Add the bay leaf and the salt. Taste for seasoning. Cover the pot and place it in the oven and bake for approximately 20 minutes, or until all of the liquid is absorbed. Remove the pot from the oven. Remove the bay leaf. Fluff the rice with a fork. Serve warm with your favorite meal.

SALATA ME KOTOPOULO TIS SKARAS

Greek Salad with Grilled Chicken

Serves 4 to 6

This is a perfect salad for a lunch or light supper. For a particularly delicious variation, try grilled shrimp or salmon.

§ § § § § §

For the Marinade:

3 tablespoons olive oil

3 tablespoons fresh squeezed lemon juice

Salt and pepper to taste

1 teaspoon dried Greek oregano

For the Chicken:

3 skinless, boneless chicken cutlets (about 1 to 1/2 pounds), rinsed and patted dry

For the Salad:

1 head romaine lettuce, sliced in half lengthwise, cut into bite-size pieces, rinsed and spun dried in a salad spinner

2 large ripe tomatoes cut into chunky wedges

1 medium cucumber, preferably seedless, peeled and sliced into chunky rounds

Greek Salad Dressing (see page 133)

1/2 pound imported Greek feta cheese, cut into wedges

1 small red onion, halved and thinly sliced

6 to 8 pepperochini peppers

6 to 8 Kalamata olives

§ § § § § §

Make the Marinade: Combine the olive oil, lemon, salt, pepper, and oregano in a small bowl and whisk well.

Make the Chicken: Preheat the grill or broiler. Place the chicken on a baking sheet. Add the marinade and turn to coat the chicken using tongs. Place the chicken on the grill or directly on the grate or broiler platter under the broiler platter under the broiler. Grill or broil the chicken for 4 to 5 minutes to produce grill marks on one side. Turn and grill or broil for 4 to 5 minutes more, depending upon the thickness until the meat is firm when touched and springs back quickly when pressed with a finger. Remove the chicken from the grill or broiler and set aside to cool. Cut the chicken into thin strips.

Make the salad: Combine the romaine, tomatoes, and cucumbers in a large bowl. Add the salad dressing and toss gently to coat. Place the salad on individual salad dishes. Divide the chicken and arrange on top of each salad. Top each salad with a wedge of cheese. Garnish with the onions, pepperochini, and olives. Serve accompanied by a glass of Robolla wine.

PAIDAKIA TIS SKARAS

Grilled Lamb Chops

Serves 4

Grilled lamb chops are a favorite at all Greek tavernas. For this simple recipe marinate the lamb chops with lemon and olive oil and put them on the grill at your next barbeque, or place them in the broiler at home. Sprinkle them with oregano after they are cooked so that the oregano doesn't burn. Serve accompanied by fried or roasted potatoes and a delicious Greek salad.

§ § § § §

2 to 2 1/2 pounds loin or rib lamb chops

Latho-Lemono Dressing (see page 121)

Salt and pepper to taste

1 teaspoon dried Greek oregano

1 lemon, cut into wedges

§ § § § §

Heat the grill or broiler. Place the lamb chops in a large baking sheet. Add the dressing and turn to coat the lamb chops using tongs. Place the lamb chops on the grill or directly on the grate of the broiler pan under the broiler. Grill or broil the lamb chops for 4 to 5 minutes, to produce grill marks on one side. Turn and grill or broil for 4 to 5 minutes more, (medium rare: 130˚ to 140˚F), or until the desired doneness. Remove the lamb chops from the broiler or grill and place on a serving platter. Sprinkle with oregano. Garnish with lemon wedges and serve immediately.

Baklava Tseis Kaik

Baklava Cheese Cake

Serves 8 to 10

The ancient Greeks made cheese cakes and sweetened them with honey. Here's a Greek inspired cheesecake that is perfect for entertaining your friends. It's a rich and creamy cheesecake topped with layers of flakey phyllo pastry and a baklava topping of crushed walnuts, cinnamon and spice. Begin making this dessert a day ahead.

§ § § § § §

1/4 pound (1 stick) unsalted butter, melted, plus 3 tablespoons
1 cup crushed walnuts
1/2 teaspoon cinnamon
1/2 teaspoon ground clove
1 1/2 cups cookie crumbs (graham crackers or vanilla wafers)
2 pounds cream cheese (preferably Philadelphia), softened
1 cup sugar
1 cup ricotta cheese
4 eggs
1/4 cup lemon juice
2 teaspoons vanilla
10 sheets phyllo pastry, (preferably fresh) sold at Greek and ethnic specialty stores
4 tablespoons Simple Syrup (see page 95)

§ § § § § §

Brush the sides and the bottom of a 9-inch, round or square, spring form pan with 3 tablespoons of the butter. Line the bottom and the sides of the pan with aluminum foil. In a medium size bowl combine the walnuts, cinnamon, and clove and set aside. In another medium size bowl, combine the cookies and remaining butter and blend together. Coat the bottom and the sides of the pan with the cookie mixture. Preheat the oven to 350F. In a large bowl, beat the cream cheese with an electric mixer until smooth, about 5 minutes. Add the sugar and beat to incorporate completely. Add the ricotta cheese and mix on low speed until well blended. Add the eggs, one at a time, beating well after each addition. Stir in the lemon and the vanilla. Pour the batter into the prepared pan. Cut the phyllo sheets into rounds or squares the size of the bottom of the pan. With the remaining butter, brush and layer the remaining 5 sheets of the phyllo. Spread the walnut mixture over top. Brush and layer the remaining phyllo rounds.

Score and place the pan into a larger baking pan. Carefully pour enough water to a depth of 1 inch of the pan. Bake for approximately 1 hour 50 minutes, or until the cake is lightly golden and firm when lightly touched in the center of the cake. Carefully remove the cake from the oven and place on a baking rack to cool completely. When completely cooled, drizzle the cake with the warm syrup. Remove the foil and place the cake into the refrigerator to cool completely, about 24 hours. When ready to serve cut into slices and place on pretty dessert dishes. Enjoy with a cup of coffee.

Variation: To make cherry cheese cake, omit the baklava topping. Bake the cake according to the recipe above. When the cake is cooled completely, top with canned cherries.

CPSIA information can be obtained
at www.ICGtesting.com
227643LV00008B